MAGIC MOMENTS FROM THE MOVIES

MAGIC MOMENTS from the MOVIES

by

Elwy Yost

DOUBLEDAY CANADA LIMITED, TORONTO, ONTARIO
DOUBLEDAY & COMPANY, INC., GARDEN CITY, NEW YORK
1978

Library of Congress Cataloging in Publication Data

Yost, Elwy.
Magic moments from the movies.

Includes index.
1. Moving-pictures—Miscellanea.   I. Title.
PN1995.Y6   791.43'09
ISBN: 0-385-13691-9
Library of Congress Catalog Card Number: 77-25615
Copyright © 1978 by Elwy Yost

This book is for Lila Ragnhild
with love

CONTENTS

⊙◎◈◎◈◎◈◎◈◎◈◎◈◎◈◎◈◎◈◎◈◎◈◎

Preface

Magic Moments is the result of a lifetime love affair with the movies. It is not so much a history of film—although it has been arranged in a chronological order—as it is more or less a random sampling of tidbits and snippets of films. Like the "grab bags" I used to buy for a penny at the little candy store next door to the theater I attended in the early thirties, so this book is a grab bag of memories of the scenes and shots, the sequences, the movie moments that most impressed me down through the years. What you are about to embark upon here is a nostalgic tour and, because I have not been able to re-screen or re-see at film festivals or on television late shows every *single* movie recorded here, one that is necessarily subject to the curious frailties of human memory. More than once on television or at film revivals I have discovered a favorite scene not to be quite the same scene I had remembered and talked about over the intervening twenty or thirty years.

The most recent illustration of this occurred when I saw *Life Begins at Eight-Thirty* (1942) on TV a few months ago. For thirty-five years I had remembered a line of Monty Woolley's delivered near the beginning of the film while he was playing Santa Claus in a large department store. The line has always been my favorite and I have regaled countless friends with it at parties. The situation is this: Woolley is a retired Shakespearean actor who each year dons a magnificent Santa Claus costume and, resplendent in beard, boots, and tassel, mounts the fabled yuletide chair in a Macy's-styled establishment to greet the kiddies. Prior to this scene, he has alighted from a limousine sent to fetch him, has "snubbed" a street-corner Salvation Army Santa whose beard and garb are not quite up to snuff, has entered a bar next to the store, and has had the bartender pour Bourbon into a hot water bottle he has brought along for the occasion. He has then stuffed this bottle into the "tummy" of his jacket and affixed a length of rubber tubing to it that is also hidden from view. Now he enters his Christmas domain and takes his position in the chair upon a dais-cum-ramp.

The kids move by in an endless line-up while Santa pats their heads and exchanges puerile pleasantries and the large crowd of parents looks on. Then the camera shows the hands of the department store clock rotating round and round to illustrate the passage of time. It stops at 3. Cut to Monty Woolley, who holds up his hands to temporarily halt the flow of kids before him and to indicate a much-needed respite. This done, he proceeds to pull the end of the rubber tube from his jacket and to insert it into his mouth. Then, arms folded, he sits back in his chair and sucks . . . and sucks . . . and sucks. The parents begin to register a mild alarm; the children at the head of the line-up who are practically touching his lap stare up, solemn and wide-eyed, into a bearded face that is engaged in the process of consuming a quart of Bourbon through a rubber tube connected to a hidden hot water bottle. Finally Woolley withdraws the tube, looks at it, burps, puts it away. Then, as a silence pervades the entire room, he bends over, looks down at the young faces before him, and says with seasonal relish: "I hate you . . . I hate you . . . I hate you."

And that is my memory of a great screen moment.

But when I saw the film on TV a few months ago, alas, it wasn't quite that way. Everything that I described in the early stages of the sequence was the same—the limousine, the Salvation Army Santa, the bar, the hot water bottle, the tubing, the store, the yuletide throne—but there was no line-up of children, there was no clock with hands turning, and worst of all, there was no "I hate you . . . I hate you . . . I hate you." Instead Woolley is pictured poised on his throne, with hat askew and legs draped over one arm of his chair, sucking on his tubing and staring out at a large crowd of rather startled adults, uttering lines of inebriated nonsense which he climaxes with, "My name is Adam Hall . . . and I hate you one and all!" Unless the scene I described a moment ago existed in the print I saw in '42 and was later edited out (which seems unlikely), it would appear I had refashioned the experience over the years into something that was more *me* than *it*. All of us do this all the time in everyday life, altering real events into versions that only partially resemble the truth. Perhaps no truly objective history of anything is ever possible.

I am not trying to suggest that the movie memories I have recorded in this book are all blighted with mental fabrication. In most instances I have either been able to re-screen the films and compare sightings with the draft notes for this book, or I have had source data to rely upon—material I had personally written in film diaries when I originally saw the movies referred to. But, in selection and description, some of the moments that appear here may well be at variance with the reader's memory, not to mention his choice and taste. Since the whole process of viewing motion pictures in darkened auditoriums, and the critical assessments and judgments we exercise in doing so is such a private experience, this work must be regarded as an unabashedly personal look at the movies. I only hope that you will enjoy reading the book as much as I enjoyed writing it.

ACKNOWLEDGMENTS

Books are "team" creations in the sense that movies and television productions are. They are never the product of lone individuals, and this work is certainly no exception. I have a number of people to thank and I want to do this now with warmth and affection.

I want to thank my father, Elwy, and my mother, Josephine, for letting me recount to them the plots of almost every movie I saw back in the thirties and forties in Weston, Ontario, and for giving me the dimes to see those movies.

I want to thank the late, great critic Nathan Cohen for hiring me to write movie reviews for the Toronto *Star* during the summer of '59 and thus letting me know my words could sell.

I want to thank my wife, Lila Ragnhild, for suggesting the concept of this book to me five years ago, and my sons, Christopher and Graham, for constantly discussing movies with me.

I want to thank Arnold Edinborough for pointing me in the direction of Doubleday, Alex Barris for directing me to the sources of photographs, and Bruce Pittman for motoring me there.

I want to thank my editor, Rick Archbold, for his faith, enthusiasm, friendship, and constant help in making this book become a reality.

And finally, I want to thank my Aunt Georgy, who used to pick me up after school in her big Durante and whisk me off to first-run pictures in movie palaces in Toronto and afterward treat me to chocolate sodas.

MAGIC MOMENTS FROM THE MOVIES

The Beginnings

From the moment a steam engine plunged toward audiences from a screen in a rented hall in New York in 1896 and emptied the first fifteen rows, the cinema clearly established itself as a medium of excitement, motion, and a sensation which seemed as immediate as reality. The picture was called *The Empire State Express* and it was one of several action shorts being presented on that occasion by one of the earliest film outfits on record, the American Biograph Company.

One year before, 1895, in France, Louis and Auguste Lumière had shared honors with the United States in giving the world the first public exhibition of motion pictures. The films were all short subjects depicting simple everyday events with such titles as *Arrival of Train at Station*. The American premiere was created by Woodville Latham and his sons and consisted of a boxing match between two illustrious figures of the day, Young Griffo and Battling Barnett. It had been shot on the roof of New York's Madison Square Garden.

For those interested in movie history, the very first evidence I could find of a series of pictures put in sequence onto a strip of film occurred in 1889. W. K. L. Dickson produced the film and

Thomas A. Edison shot it on a base provided by George (Kodak) Eastman. The scene showed three men grooming a horse.

So much for the very start of things. But when, in France in 1902, Georges Méliès fired his first manned rocket into space (*Voyage to the Moon*) and began to devise double exposures, dissolves, and fade-outs, the cinema became a place of fantasy and imagination. A year later, in 1903, when Edwin S. Porter in the U.S.A. gave us *The Great Train Robbery*—albeit only one ten-minute reel in length—the screen began to tell stories with a beginning, middle, and end. And when, in 1909, *Gertie the Dinosaur* crossed the screen, the animated cartoon was born.

By 1907, what was now a galloping new art industry included, apart from Edison, such companies as Biograph, Vitagraph, Méliès, Kalem, Lubin, Thanhouser, and Essanay and Selig. The latter two were Chicago-based, but most companies of the time were located in New York, with the exception of Lubin, which hailed from Philadelphia. Their studios were small by today's standards, were open-aired to utilize the sunlight, and, because movies were silent, permitted the filming of several one- and two-reelers in adjacent stalls or booths at the same time. The very first studio was called the Black Maria and was constructed in West Orange, New Jersey, in 1893 for the princely sum of $637.67. Initially it was used for the making of materials for such peep-show devices of the day as Kinetoscopes and Mutoscopes, which were hand-operated machines that created an illusion of motion through rapidly moving still pictures on film strips and on cards.

In the early years and almost up to World War I, the names of the actors and actresses that appeared in films were not included in the credits. The concept of stars and star appeal was unknown at the time. No one had thought of it, no one pushed for it and, besides, the producers were not about to urge the implementation of anything that would give rise to demands for higher salaries. But the public began to develop attachments for certain regular performers, and so by 1908 a certain sixteen-year-old named Gladys Smith from Toronto became known as "Little Mary," from the characters she played, long before the public knew her as Mary Pickford. At Biograph, exquisitely lovely Florence Lawrence was known as "the Biograph Girl." It was not until the 1910–13 period that Carl Laemmle of I.M.P. (Independent Motion Picture Company—later Universal) saw the monetary advantages to advertising certain players in certain pictures—and the "star system" was born. Florence Lawrence was invited to join I.M.P. at $1,000 a week and became the first modern star.

Among the favorites of those early years were Charles Chaplin, Douglas Fairbanks, Sr., William S. Hart, Ken Maynard, Tom Mix, Art Acord, Francis X. Bushman, Mabel Normand, Thomas Meighan, King Baggott, Henry B. Walthall, Mary Philbin, Bebe Daniels, Constance Talmadge, Fatty Arbuckle, Harold Lloyd, Mack Sennett's Keystone Cops, and, in 1919, Lon Chaney for his work in *The Miracle Man.*

In 1914 Charlie Chaplin's salary was $150 per week; by 1916 it was $1,250 per week. Studios were expanding to satisfy the growing public appetite for movies, and movies were becoming longer. In 1913 Cecil B. DeMille produced North America's first feature-length film, *The Squaw Man,* in a fig, apricot, and citrus ranch area of Los Angeles called Hollywood to which, by now, the focus of motion picture production had pretty well shifted. Movies were swiftly becoming a large and viable industry, a highly profitable big business, but it was a man named David Wark Griffith who, by 1915 and 1916, with such pictures as *The Birth of a Nation* and *Intolerance,* became that industry's first artist and innovator.

It was between 1908 and 1915, in one- and two-reelers, that he dared to disembody such performers as Lillian Gish by shooting a close-up so that only the face would fill the screen. He began cross-cutting in mid-action from one scene to another, using a variety of camera angles and distances from his subject within single scenes, coupling extreme long shots with extreme close shots, and freeing his camera from a fixed position so that it could track or dolly after moving people and objects, and employing fade-outs to terminate scenes. Through these innovations the basic syntax of the modern motion picture was invented.

THE BIRTH OF A NATION, 1915

Henry B. Walthall raises his sword atop a sandbagged firing line and charges in David Wark Griffith's *The Birth of a Nation* and the camera backtracks, keeping Walthall in close medium distance as he runs toward us, picking up a flag as he goes, war and death and destruction all around him. The run is not long, but the camera makes it the archetype of all heroic runs against impossible odds in time of battle.

INTOLERANCE, 1916

⊚⊚⊚⊚⊚⊚⊚⊚⊚⊚⊚⊚⊚⊚⊚⊚⊚⊚⊚⊚⊚⊚

The climax of *Intolerance*, Griffith's masterpiece, contains some of the most dramatic editing in film history. The viewer has been observing, for over two screen hours, the development of four parallel stories, three historical, one modern, depicting man's inhumanity to man.

The modern tale is set against a background of labor unrest and shows the process by which a young man is arrested for a murder which he did not commit, is tried, found guilty, and imprisoned to await execution on the state scaffold. All the while his mother, who believes in his innocence, is attempting to procure the necessary evidence to have him freed. This story is intercut with the three historical tales: the expulsion of the Huguenots from France, Christ's last days and crucifixion, and the fall of Babylon. As *Intolerance* advances, the parallel story segments get shorter until, in the climax, Griffith cuts from century to century in a maelstrom of editing acrobatics, the segments running barely a few seconds each, some fragments of seconds.

It is here that my favorite screen cross-cut occurs: in one blinding cinematic moment we cut from Christ being nailed to the cross at Calvary to a train roaring across twentieth-century America, a train carrying the governor of a state who is the only man who can stop the execution of the factory worker, a train pursued by an open touring car bearing the mother of the condemned man who now has the proof of her son's innocence. That is the moment, imperishable, magnificent among all moments. But the picture charges forward relentlessly toward its conclusion. The young man is now upon the state scaffold and has the black hood and the noose placed around his neck. Huguenots are

5

slaughtered in the streets of Paris, the nailing of Christ's arms and feet to the cross continues, and chariots roar along the walls of ancient Babylon.

We know what happened in history—Christ's death, the fall of Babylon, the extinction of the Huguenots—but in the modern tale there is ultimately a more positive note. The boy's mother catches up to the train, speaks to the governor, and, just as the trap door is about to be sprung in the prison, the execution is halted. In a final scene we see two warring armies symbolically laying down their rifles and advancing toward and embracing each other.

Intolerance was a financial failure. It was too much for audiences of its day, who did not comprehend, for instance, the story segment "interlocking" device that Griffith used whereby Lillian Gish rocked a cradle accompanied by Walt Whitman's lines: "Out of the cradle endlessly rocking . . ." But critically it was then, as it still remains, a landmark in motion picture history. In it was much, if not all, of the basic grammar of film making for the next half century.

JUDEX, 1917

⊚⊚⊚⊚⊚⊚⊚⊚⊚⊚⊚⊚⊚⊚⊚⊚⊚⊚⊚⊚⊚⊚⊚

One evening several years ago at a film society showing I had the unique pleasure of watching all twelve chapters of Feuillade's serial, *Judex* (a French precursor to The Shadow), strung out end to end in a four-hour continuum. Horace Lapp handled the piano, improvising the moods of the melodrama with panache.

In one of many climactic moments, Judex's aides storm the top suite of a seven-story apartment building where kidnappers are holding a tiny baby for ransom. The baby, in one of the most incredulous and gasping moments in screen history, is dropped over the side of a balcony by one of the aides. It falls all the way toward the pavement far below, *but* . . . a waiting Judex plus accomplice catch the little nipper in a blanket, hop into a waiting car, and speed off.

SHOULDER ARMS, 1918

In *Shoulder Arms*, Charles Chaplin is preparing for bed in a trench dugout compartment that has so much rain water in it, the bed is completely covered. Nonchalantly, with the dignity and self-respect that have always characterized his tramp character, he reaches below the surface of the water, produces his pillow, by now a wet blob, "puffs" it out the way people do when they make their beds, then replaces it below the surface of the water. He nexts lights a candle which stands on a piece of floating wood so that he can read his drenched newspaper before going to sleep. This scene reaches its peak when the wood bearing the lighted candle drifts slowly across the room toward the large toes of the sergeant protruding above the water level in the opposite bunk.

THE CABINET OF DR. CALIGARI, 1919

⊚⊚⊚⊚⊚⊚⊚⊚⊚⊚⊚⊚⊚⊚⊚⊚⊚⊚⊚⊚⊚⊚⊚

One of the great pictorial moments from silent days occurs in Robert Wiene's bizarre *The Cabinet of Dr. Caligari,* generally regarded as the first sophisticated horror movie ever made.

Shot in close, confining studio spacial areas with angular, stylized sets, *Caligari* emerges as a claustrophobic world of narrow twisted streets and wildly leaning walls and lampposts. In my favorite moment somnambulist-monster Conrad Veidt is shown carrying lovely Lil Dagover, draped listlessly in his arms, along the peak of a crazy rooftop. Following two vicious murders executed at the command of the mad doctor of the title, Veidt had been sent to kill Miss Dagover but has succumbed to her beauty and has decided instead to kidnap her.

Pursued by townspeople, he is trying to escape over the neighboring buildings, all jumbled together in wild architectural confusion. The starkness of the pair against the wash of sky, she attired totally in white and he in black, the suspense of the scene and the mood of foreboding generated by the horrors already projected by the story up to this point, the expressionistic rooftop decor which suggests irrationality and insanity, the slow automated movements of Veidt, and the sublime languor of Dagover—these combine to infuse the moment with graphic vividness and an extraordinary mood of the baroque and the eerie.

9

The Twenties

Between the Versailles Treaty of 1919 and the stock market crash of 1929, North American society underwent dramatic changes. The automobile finally, and irrevocably, replaced the horse and buggy, and traffic jams were born. Cities began to spread out along auto routes. Radio arrived, advertising boomed, and the jazz age dawned. The motion picture industry, which was number five on the continent at the beginning of the twenties, rose to number four position by the end of the period. And the silent film, more than twenty years in birth and development when World War I finished, met an untimely death in the last few years of the decade on the very eve of the complete fulfillment of its style and technique.

Its killer—sound!

But what a decade it was up until that time! And not only in America but in other parts of the world. In Germany Fritz Lang made *Metropolis* and *Doktor Mabuse der Spieler* and, together with other directors and technicians, developed a more complex use of lighting that allowed for a greater range of mood and atmosphere on the screen. In the U.S.S.R. Sergei Eisenstein made *Potemkin* and carried editing and montage to new heights of perfection. And in France, on the very eve of the "sound" revolution, Abel Gance made a five-hour silent epic called *Napoleon* which anticipated the Cinerama process of the fifties with three screens of synchronized action. He let the camera do everything including stand on its head. In one scene, depicting a snowball fight at a school when Napoleon was a young boy, the camera is actually "thrown" to simulate the effects of a snowball in flight. In another scene it "becomes" a guillotine blade . . . and falls . . . and cuts. But *Napoleon* was judged to be too revolutionary, coming as it did at the advent of another revolution—sound—and never received the exposure it merited.

In America the decade started off with the marriage of Mary Pickford and Douglas Fairbanks. Pickford made *Pollyanna* that same year and Fairbanks made *The Mollycoddle* for director Victor Fleming, followed by *The Mark of Zorro*, a movie that established the actor's swashbuckling style for the rest of his days. Pearl White thrilled audiences with *The Perils of Pauline*, a serial that was so successful it firmly established that episodic format and genre—actually in existence since *What Happened to Mary* in 1913—for over thirty years to come. And Lon Chaney added to his laurels with *The Penalty*.

With the star system firmly entrenched in the movie industry, the setting was perfect for the coming of Rudolph Valentino in 1921 in *The Four Horsemen of the Apocalypse*, based on the famous Blasco Ibañez novel. Valentino then starred in *The Sheik* and *Blood and Sand*, and the three pictures catapulted the actor into a kind of adulation that is still remembered more than half a century later.

The decade saw many notable films: *Robin Hood*, which utilized enormous sets on the Pickford-Fairbanks United Artists lot in Santa Monica; Cecil B. DeMille's *The Ten Commandments*, with its spectacular parting of the Red Sea; *The Covered Wagon*, directed by James Cruze and shot on an eight-week location stint in Snake Valley, Nevada; *The Salvation Hunters*, which began the career of Josef von Sternberg; *The Iron Horse* by director John Ford; Chaplin's *The Gold Rush; Greed*, directed by Eric von Stroheim; *Wings*, directed by William A. Wellman, with Gary Cooper, Clara Bow, and Richard Arlen; Buster Keaton's *The General; Ben Hur*, with Francis X. Bushman and Ramon Novarro; and F. W. Murnau's brilliant *Sunrise*, starring George O'Brien and Janet Gaynor and based on the Hermann Sudermann novel *A Trip to Tilsit*.

In 1927–28 the Academy of Motion Picture Arts and Sciences conferred a new status on the entire industry when it inaugurated the annual Academy Awards. Janet Gaynor was the first actress to win, for best performances in *Seventh Heaven, Street Angel*, and *Sunrise*. Emil Jannings was voted best actor for *The Last Command* and *The Way of All Flesh*. And Frank Borzage and Lewis Milestone shared directorial honors for, respectively, *Seventh Heaven* and *Two Arabian Knights*.

But it is probably for its technical achievements that the decade will be most remembered. In *The Phantom of the Opera* (1925)—a black-and-white film as were all the others of the period—a single scene was actually shot in color. Two years earlier, DeMille had tried the technique in one sequence of *The Ten Commandments*, and the same year a process known as Prizmacolour was used for the British historical film *The Great Adventure*. And tinting and hand-colored stenciling went back to 1898. But the color effects in that one scene in *Phantom* were really quite startling for the time and deserve special mention here. In 1924 *The Thief of Bagdad*, starring Douglas Fairbanks, Sr., was accompanied in its release by a recording of background music which had been composed by Mortimer Wilson, one of the earliest examples on record of music being created for the screen by a distinguished composer. And *The Lost World* (1925), featuring Wallace Beery, Bessie Love, and Lloyd Hughes, gave Willis O'Brien, special effects engineer, the time of his life (next to *King Kong*) animating, frame by frame, inanimate models of prehistoric monsters in table-top South American jungles.

Then, in 1927, came sound.

The Jazz Singer, produced by Warner Brothers and starring Al Jolson, opened on October 6, 1927, and made film history. Actually a good part of the film was silent, but the scenes that counted were in sound. Audiences loved what they heard, and the silent film as a popular art form was dead. Warners named the new process Vitaphone. It consisted of a wax recording of the actors' voices and sound effects synchronized to the film projector. Later, sound was put optically right onto the film—the system used today—but for its time, and despite obvious defects, Vitaphone was a remarkably innovative technique.

The careers of actors and actresses were affected almost overnight. Bad voices were out and good voices were in, with a resulting surge of talent from Broadway to L.A. Voice coaching became de rigueur for many whose vocal assets lay somewhere between the aforementioned extremes. In some cases the lack of refinement of early sound recording systems in the studios tragically altered the careers of eminent silent stars, the instance of John Gilbert being one of the more notable. Ironically, motion picture technique suffered until into the early thirties because cameras had to be encased in sound booths to muffle their inherent noises, thus rendering them immobile. But sound persisted, and other techniques simply had to adjust to accommodate it.

A word now about the studios themselves in the twenties, their expansions and their mergers. United Artists, which had been formed in 1919 by Fairbanks, Pickford, and Chaplin (prompting one pundit of the day to exclaim: "The inmates have taken over the asylum"), flourished, as did Universal, Fox, and Paramount, which were already well established. RKO came into being in 1921 as the result of an RCA Keith-Orpheum circuit merger, and in 1924 Harry Cohn personally founded Columbia. The Brothers Warner joined forces in 1923, creating the colossus that still bears their name. In 1920 Loew's Incorporated, an exhibiting concern, bought into Metro Pictures and in 1924 merged with the Goldwyn production company, although Sam Goldwyn immediately left and set up his own independent enterprise. Then, in 1925, Louis B. Mayer joined the group and what we know today as M-G-M (Metro-Goldwyn-Mayer) was officially christened.

It was thus mainly in the twenties, through mergers between motion picture production companies and film exhibition systems, that a powerfully profitable foundation was built, welding together both the product and the means of distribution of that product, and it would contribute immeasurably to the growth of the American film industry for the next thirty years.

14

WAY DOWN EAST, 1920

Richard Barthelmess dashes out across a moving ice floe to rescue Lillian Gish from certain death in the ending of D. W. Griffith's *Way Down East*. What grabs one's attention during the viewing of this passage, and what burns the sequence into the mind for years and years to come, is the total reality of it: the river is real, the ice is real, and the actors are really out there: the girl huddled like a lump of old clothes to her ice cake watching the falls get closer and closer, the young man doggedly pursuing her for miles, finally leaping from cake to cake, the weight of his body forcing the cakes to bob and dip, almost losing his balance a dozen times as he works his uncertain way closer and closer to the girl. And then, on the very lip of the waterfall, Barthelmess makes his last desperate leap to the ice cake his beloved is stranded upon, sweeps her up in his arms, and as the cake glides over the brink of the cascade, begins to hop, skip, and jump his way back upstream to shore and safety.

GREED, 1924

⊚⊚⊚⊚⊚⊚⊚⊚⊚⊚⊚⊚⊚⊚⊚⊚⊚⊚⊚⊚⊚

Greed is Eric von Stroheim's masterpiece even though the released version is several hours shorter than the original. (The released version is about three hours long as it is, and this is still a lot of *Greed.*) Legend has it that Stroheim wanted to release the nine-hour picture on a single, day-long, showing basis, but that Adolph Zukor would have none of this. June Mathis was assigned to do the cutting; it took her nearly a year, and the results are wonderful.

Best of all is the ending, awesomely imaginative in its tragic irony. McTeague (Gibson Gowland) is a dentist who is driven nearly mad by the penny-pinching obsessiveness of Trina, his wife (Zasu Pitts), and finally he murders her. Taking the $5,000 in coins that his wife has been hoarding, plus her caged canary and other possessions, he takes flight across the great salt flats of Death Valley pursued by Marcus (Jean Hersholt), an old friend and Trina's former beau, who is now a sheriff and who knows about the small fortune McTeague is carrying.

Marcus catches up with McTeague at his encampment in the middle of the salt wasteland, arrests him, and handcuffs himself to his quarry. Then they start to fight. Pounding each other mercilessly, they roll over and over in the salt until McTeague gains an advantage and, with one hand, strangles Marcus. Then he searches in the dead man's pockets for the key to the handcuffs, but he cannot find it. Desperately he starts to claw at the loose salt; still he cannot locate the key. And because of Marcus' weight (he is a man of no little size) he is unable to move any distance to continue his search. In fact, he is anchored to the spot.

And so he sits beside the dead body of his once close friend, his water gone, his horse having fled, the little canary dead in its cage, staring at the dismal vastness around him and awaiting the end.

THE PHANTOM OF THE OPERA, 1925

When Mary Philbin first haltingly, hesitatingly, fearfully crept up behind the mad Erik (Lon Chaney, Sr.) in *The Phantom of the Opera* and jerked off his mask, the world gasped in horror. Audiences still do whenever this sequence is reshown. A combination of gradual suspense, shock, and gorgeously grisly makeup (stark round eyes with piercing pupils, the open mouth revealing crooked, decaying teeth, the flattened, flaring nostrils, the whole face resembling a ghastly slab of Roquefort cheese) make this moment a match for any in a modern horror film.

POTEMKIN, 1925

Scrgci Eisenstein in *Potemkin* commits to film some of the opening orchestrations of the Russian Revolution. His focus on the naval and dockyard strikes in Odessa circa 1903 permits him to interpret with bravura the famous episode on the steps where Czarist soldiers gunned down dozens of civilians.

The editing is extraordinarily quick—in fact, the film hits its stride early, with few shots exceeding the count of "three"—and develops a terrifying rhythm in which successive tiers of white-uniformed troops march in dreadful mechanization down the steps, sweeping everything before them. The camera cuts from the synchronization of their moving limbs to the smoke from their discharging rifles to the legs of civilians buckling beneath them, in short shots, many only a fraction of a second long. In one startling close-up the lens in a woman's glasses splinters and blood gushes from her eye socket.

This picture ranks with *Sunrise* (which I'll get to in a moment) as the zenith of expressiveness in the silent film, a totally visual form that really had to be experienced within the context of the silent era for a full appreciation of its special language. That this motion picture communicates so effectively today after four decades of sound is a tribute to Eisenstein's sculptural genius on the silver screen.

THE GOLD RUSH, 1925

My father told me about the big scene in *The Gold Rush* when I was very little, and he must have told it to me over and over again. But it was not until a revival of the film in 1948, complete with a musical and sound-effects background, that I finally saw it.

The now legendary scene concerns Chaplin's almost total destitution in a lonely little cabin in the Klondike. Finally reduced to consuming his own clothing, Chaplin boils his boots and prepares to eat them in a scene commingling abject poverty and despair with the table manners of a French gourmet. To watch Chaplin picking and chewing with great deftness and delicacy the leather from around the sole of one of his boots, a napkin stuffed properly in his tattered waist jacket, his eyes blankly staring at us while his mouth performs all the acrobatics necessary for the task, then finally detecting, somewhere in his mouth, the presence of a nail, finding it, tossing it away with a "clunk," then resuming his repast, is to observe the stuff of timeless art.

THE BLACK PIRATE, 1926

In *The Black Pirate* Douglas Fairbanks, Sr., leaps from a spar high up in the rigging of a Spanish galleon onto the ship's mainsail and, jabbing his dagger into the canvas, slices his way down the sail to the decking dozens of feet below. The moment is a delicious flight of fancy and human acrobatics and typifies the flair Fairbanks brought to the screen.

Later in the same film he singlehandedly takes over an entire vessel from enemy hands, dueling at one time with as many as fifteen men, occasionally doing a front flip somersault over their heads, then quickly disarming them from the rear before they can get turned around. The fact that he performed feats like these over and over again with a dashing smile and aristocratic aplomb made him one of the legends of the movies.

SUNRISE, 1927

⊚①②③④⑤⑥⑦⑧⑨⑩⑪⑫⑬⑭⑮⑯⑰⑱⑲⑳

F. W. Murnau's *Sunrise* is set in some unnamed European country during the early years of this century. The film contrasts rural and urban life through a near-tragic love triangle that depicts how the idyllic life of a country man and woman (George O'Brien and Janet Gaynor) is destroyed when the man becomes so smitten by an urban vamp that he contemplates drowning his wife. The sequence that has always boggled my mind for its sheer cinematic imagination relates, however, to one of the less turbulent passages of the film—a tram ride from the country to the city.

Janet Gaynor boards the tram—the ride starts at the end of the line in a wooded area by a lake where the streetcar makes a loop in preparation for its return trip to the city—and the camera boards with her, occupying a position immediately behind and to one side of her with its focus out through the front windows. The tram becomes mobile and the camera never alters its position throughout the entire ride into town. The result is a moving camera or track shot of such incredible dexterity that one marvels at ordinary, everyday sights and images as though observing them for the first time. Trees give way to factories, shops, verandas, and assorted house fronts as the tram rounds curve after curve, each bend revealing new homes and structures in greater density.

I discovered only recently that Murnau erected all of these buildings in a studio lot in order to achieve the precise sense of transition and community that he felt *Sunrise* demanded.

The Thirties

The thirties, that somewhat plain-spoken period of the Great Depression which ended with the outbreak of World War II, saw the factory or studio system dominate the motion picture industry and carry it to unprecedented heights of power and wealth. In my preface to the twenties I mentioned a key feature of that system, the union of the means of production and distribution under single studio control. This was mainly done through mergers, sometimes through straight acquisitions. The most notable example of this process in the thirties occurred in 1935 when Joseph Schenck's Twentieth Century Pictures merged with William Fox's Fox Film Corporation, which, incidentally, controlled a vast theater exhibition chain. Darryl F. Zanuck, one of the most genuinely creative of all cinema czars, became production chief of the newly formed enterprise and remained in that post for more than twenty consecutive years.

But the expression "factory system" implies something else, and I refer here to the corporate structures of the eight majors—Warners, Metro, Columbia, Fox, Paramount, RKO, Universal, and United Artists—and to their methods of operation.

They were run by tough bosses who exercised a tight control

over every phase of their operations but who paid lavishly to procure the best talent in the world, on screen and behind it, to make their pictures. Their studios were set up no differently than companies in the automotive industry or the clothing industry. They were composed of a network of separate departments, each one formed in terms of its own specialty—properties, costumes, editing, sound recording, cinematography, special effects, etc.— and each was fused to the central command, the studio head, and accountable to him, through a system of supervisors and department heads. Zanuck, for example, used associate producers to execute all his orders, and was thus able to keep a moment-by-moment account of the progress of every major phase and aspect of every ongoing production. But what I want to emphasize here is the system of specialty departments. On a guided tour through M-G-M ten years ago, my family and I were shown into a warehouse containing nothing but stairs—hundreds of stairs and steps of every imaginable description, from stairs one would associate with a southern plantation of the last century to those one might have expected to find in the corner of a trench in World War I. It was my wife who exclaimed, "My God, this place is a factory . . . it's all a great big factory!" And so it was.

The end product may sometimes have been art, but the methods were hard, lean, and pragmatic. And much of the success of the factory system was due to this. Even the actors were properties, tied by long-term contracts to their studio's needs.

Sound and color had come to the movies in the twenties, but the thirties gave them a permanent place. Color was slower in getting a fix on the industry, but following the success of *Becky Sharp* in 1935 it gained greater momentum each year. *Wings of the Morning* in 1937 and *The Adventures of Robin Hood* in 1938 added impetus to the movement.

The low-budget or "B" picture made its appearance due to rising costs; double features became a normal procedure; and going to the movies developed into a weekly habit for about 80 million people (as against today's 18 million). While the decade opened modestly, by the end of it motion picture production had soared to the point where the major studios brought out a new feature every week, and the entire Hollywood industry, including independent movie makers, produced between four and five hundred films a year.

The year 1930 saw such films as *Anna Christie*, *The Love Parade*, and one genuine classic, *All Quiet on the Western Front*. But 1939 was a watershed year for American movies, with *Mr. Smith Goes to Washington*, *Stagecoach*, *The Wizard of Oz*, *Goodbye Mr. Chips*, *Wuthering Heights*, *Destry Rides Again*, *Ninotchka*, *Gone with the Wind*, and *Gunga Din*. And *Citizen Kane* and *The Great McGinty* were just around the corner.

On the international scene, Russia's Sergei Eisenstein was making *Alexander Nevsky* (1938); England's Alexander Korda was producing *The Scarlet Pimpernel* (1935), and Alfred Hitchcock was shooting *The Thirty-Nine Steps* the same year; France was creating the Marius trilogy, written by Marcel Pagnol, between 1931 and 1934; and Fritz Lang was making *M* in Germany, starring Peter Lorre.

In Canada in 1939 the National Film Board was founded, with its base in Ottawa, Ontario, under the guiding genius of Britain's documentary pioneer John Grierson.

Stars shone more brightly in the American firmament than in any previous decade: James Cagney, Edward G. Robinson, Jean Harlow, Hedy Lamarr, Bette Davis, Olivia De Havilland, Errol Flynn, Clark Gable, Spencer Tracy, Claudette Colbert, Cary Grant, Irene Dunne, Carole Lombard, Fredric March, Leslie Howard, Vivien Leigh, Ingrid Bergman, Walter Huston, Ronald Colman, Marlene Dietrich, Laurel and Hardy, Gary Cooper, Charles Laughton, Merle Oberon, Dorothy Lamour, Jon Hall, Douglas Fairbanks, Jr., Barbara Stanwyck, Jeanette MacDonald, Nelson Eddy, and Eddie Cantor, to name some.

The thirties were a mean, lean period but, judging from the foregoing list of luminaries, a period when dreams ran high.

THE BLUE ANGEL, 1930

Emil Jannings goes out of his mind in Josef von Sternberg's German production of *The Blue Angel* in a scene that so precariously borders on the comic that it is doubtful whether any other actor of the time could have pulled it off with such a deft blend of horror, pathos, and the madly grotesque.

A once respected high school teacher (or professor), Jannings has fallen under the seductive spell of Lola-Lola (Marlene Dietrich) and has degenerated into a brooding, drunken wreck of a man, ultimately finding himself back in his home town as part of the stage act of Dietrich's traveling cabaret, facing his old students and once close colleagues in a clown's outfit while the company magician breaks an egg over his bald head.

Crowing like a rooster and walking blindly around the stage, Jannings brings a comic-grisly revulsion to his audience and has to be subdued by a strait jacket.

Later, while snow gently falls on the midnight streets of his old town, he makes his way back to his school, where, at his desk in his empty classroom, he quietly dies.

ALL QUIET
ON THE WESTERN FRONT, 1930

◎◎◎◎◎◎◎◎◎◎◎◎◎◎◎◎◎◎◎◎◎◎◎

It is the moment of armistice, 1918, in Lewis Milestone's *All Quiet on the Western Front.* Lew Ayres reaches over the lip of his trench toward a butterfly which has briefly alighted on the ground, its presence creating an ironic counterpoint to the endless vista of mud and barrenness and death. As his fingers are about to touch the fragile creature, a sniper's bullet kills him.

CITY LIGHTS, 1931

◎◎◎◎◎◎◎◎◎◎◎◎◎◎◎◎◎◎◎◎◎◎

James Agee once declared that the last shot in Charles Chaplin's *City Lights* was the greatest ever taken in the history of movies. Agee might well be right, though he has been dead many years and a whole new cinema has arisen since his pronouncement. Certainly, within the dramatic context of the picture itself, the last shot of Chaplin's face is staggering in its impact.

The tramp has befriended a blind flower girl and has undertaken all kinds of jobs in order to raise the money for an operation that can restore her sight.

Emerging from a short term in prison, he discovers not only that she has her own flower shop but that now she can see.

In the last scene he approaches her and she sells him a flower, not knowing who he is. However, in taking the money from the palm of his hand, her sensitive touch reveals to her the identity of the comical-looking character in front of her. Recognition begins to dawn on her face. Chaplin puts the rose to his mouth and clenches the stem with his teeth. In a state of anguish and hopeful expectancy, he wonders if she will find in reality the prince of her dreams. The film fades on this moment of pathos-comedy.

FRANKENSTEIN, 1931

⊚⊚⊚⊚⊚⊚⊚⊚⊚⊚⊚⊚⊚⊚⊚⊚⊚⊚⊚⊚⊚⊚⊚⊚

When Boris Karloff, as the Monster in James Whale's version of *Frankenstein,* moved his hand for the first time after being brought down from the high tower where his fabricated body had been given a charge of lightning, the world shuddered and the American horror film had its beginning. Later in the movie when the Monster made his first "erect" entrance, Whale had him walk into a room *backward,* a brilliant touch and a very amusingly curious one.

THE VIKING, 1931

⊙⊙⊙⊙⊙⊙⊙⊙⊙⊙⊙⊙⊙⊙⊙⊙⊙⊙⊙⊙⊙⊙⊙

The Viking is largely forgotten today except by students of the Canadian cinema. Really a combined Canadian-American effort, Varick Frizzell's film is set in Newfoundland-Labrador country and focuses its lens on the annual seal hunt. The film is really a semi-documentary, setting its conflict between good guy and bad guy, and love interest, against the preparations for an execution of the hunt itself.

What remains riveted in my mind are the shots of the fur-clad hunters on the ice floes pursuing their quarry. Leaping from pan to pan, the men move across a vast expanse of broken ice, a carpet of white that undulates in the broad swells of the Atlantic. These sequences—the jumping men who stagger precariously at times, the bobbing cakes, the enormous undulation—are thrilling to behold, particularly when one realizes the action is real—it is happening—and not the work of special effects.

THE MASK OF FU MANCHU, 1932

⊙◎⊚◎⊚◎⊚◎⊚◎⊚◎⊙◎⊚◎⊚◎⊚◎⊚◎⊚◎⊙

Boris Karloff in M-G-M's *The Mask of Fu Manchu* never looked more magnificently sinister. The lighting on his Oriental face has not before or since been equaled in texture, tone, or contrast. The lighting is almost liquid in the way it runs into the lines and movements of expression, and the evil that it illuminates has an exquisite beauty that mocks and parodies all conventional morality.

One of the truly great moments in the history of cinema occurs when Karloff is standing beside the outstretched form of Lewis Stone, whom he has tied in a helpless prone position in order to torture him into revealing vital information about the location of the lost tomb of Genghis Khan. Immediately above Stone's head is a large bell. When his captive fails to respond to questions, Karloff rings the bell, and the resonant gong, far worse than Big Ben, drives Stone's brain into insane reverberations.

During pauses between gongs Karloff leans close to his victim's blazing eyes and parched lips (all food and water have been denied him) and languidly bites into a cluster of plump succulent grapes. He grins almost lovingly, his long moustaches, slanted eyes, and broad, slitted, crooked grin bestowing Satanic benediction upon his victim.

MR. ROBINSON CRUSOE, 1932

⊚⊚⊚⊚⊚⊚⊚⊚⊚⊚⊚⊚⊚⊚⊚⊚⊚⊚⊚⊚⊚

In *Mr. Robinson Crusoe* Douglas Fairbanks, Sr., is a millionaire yachtsman who wagers with a colleague that he can live for a year on a remote South Seas island they happen to be passing. The bet is accepted, the friend promises to have the boat anchored at the precise spot one year hence, and Fairbanks, accompanied by his dog, bids farewell and dives into the sea.

His year is fraught with all kinds of Crusoe-like adventures, but the climax offers a wild piece of escapist imagination, possibly the wildest in Fairbanks' screen history.

As savage cannibals commence their attack on his primitive settlement—it is one year to the day since he swam ashore—Fairbanks climbs a low launching tower he has constructed and sails off through the jungle over the heads of the clambering natives on a homemade trolley car. Clinging to the vehicle's rope structure, Fairbanks dodges arrows and spears as he flits through the shadows of the great jungle trees bound for the seashore. The scene is a marvelous flight of pure wonder. Once on the beach Fairbanks places himself in a catapult he has fashioned with two enormous palm trees winched and bent over to ground level and moored to anchor pegs by tawny vines. These he hacks at with his trusty machete. Then, as devilish natives roar in to capture him, he finally succeeds in severing the mooring vines. The giant palm trees snap erect and our hero is catapulted hundreds of yards out to sea alongside—you guessed it—the waiting yacht. He has survived and won his bet.

ECSTASY, 1933

Hedy Lamarr (Hedwig Kiesler when this Czechoslovakian film was made) swims nude in a lyrically lovely scene in *Ecstasy*, and at one point comes fairly close to the camera, then turns over on her back an inch or so below the surface of the water. The sight is quite unforgettable.

Later she runs through some woods, the camera following her as though she were a young faun and catching her nude form in fleeting, graceful, upside-down images mirrored on the surface of a passing stream.

Still later she allows a young engineer to seduce her (she is married to a man much older than herself and is in a state of extremis frustratis) and the shots of her face during this sequence remain to this day the most beautiful of their kind ever filmed. The fact that director Gustav Machaty resorted to the technique of pricking an off-screen pin into the off-screen bottom of Miss Lamarr in order to achieve little moments of delicious pain and thus contribute to the effectiveness of this sequence needn't be mentioned here.

THE INVISIBLE MAN, 1933

⊚⊚⊚⊚⊚⊚⊚⊚⊚⊚⊚⊚⊚⊚⊚⊚⊚⊚⊚⊚⊚⊚

Universal's production of the H. G. Wells novel *The Invisible Man*, starring Claude Rains in his first screen role and featuring some lovely special effects by John P. Fulton, is another example of the black humor of James Whale. The scene where Dr. Griffin (Rains) slowly unwinds a bandage from his totally invisible head, all the while badgering and mocking the village burghers who confront him, may well be the definitive moment of eerieness on the screen. But my favorite is where Rains, gradually going out of his mind as the chemical that makes him invisible begins to produce its gruesome side effects, hops, skips, and jumps along a quiet country lane, garbed only in a pair of trousers—which is all that we see on the screen—singing "Pop Goes the Weasel." It is a mad scene, a funny scene, an unearthly scene.

In another sequence, his megalomania mounting to unparalleled heights, Rains proclaims in his husky voice: "We'll start with a few murders. Big men. Little men. Just to show we make no distinction." And then: "Power! To make the world grovel at my feet. To walk into the gold vaults of nations, the chambers of kings, into the holy of holies. Even the moon is frightened of me, frightened to death. The whole world is frightened to death."

A superb speech, and another splendid moment in a great film.

KING KONG, 1933

⊚⊚⊚⊚⊚⊚⊚⊚⊚⊚⊚⊚⊚⊚⊚⊚⊚⊚⊚⊚⊚⊚

Its gargantuan star billed as the "eighth wonder of the world,"
King Kong was under the inspiration and over-all supervision of
Merian C. Cooper, the scene-by-scene direction of Ernest B.
Schoedsack, and the frame-by-frame engineering of Willis
O'Brien in its special effects sequences. The film was a team cre-
ation in every way.

It takes thirty-three minutes to bring Kong on screen, but from
the time he enters and carries away Fay Wray (she has been
tied to a stone pyre by terrified natives as a sacrificial offering to
the great ape) to his climactic fall from the top of the Empire
State Building, the outrageously horrendous thrills and the fear-
stricken screams of Fay never cease.

There are many memorable moments of adventure/fantasy in
King Kong, but the best of them all occurs near the end when
the creature is atop the Empire State Building being strafed by
the machine-gun fire of attacking aircraft. In a series of truly
bravura camera shots—moving or track shots—we, the audience,
assume the perspective of the diving planes and sweep straight
down toward the beast while he pummels his chest, roars, and
tries to reach out and snatch us right out of the sky. He succeeds
once, but mostly he misses and we shoot past, coming perilously
close to his fanged jaws and blazing eyes.

The sequence is over, and soon Kong is dead and Robert
Armstrong is saying "'Twas beauty killed the beast." But we do
not easily forget those swift, eerily jerky, engine-throbbing, animated dives.

The film abounds in great cinematic moments: the shipboard
"movie-making" sequence in which Fay is directed by Robert

Armstrong into imagining she is beholding something so monstrous and grotesque that she cannot get the screams out of her throat, then letting go, and screaming with every nerve end in her body . . . the seconds leading up to Kong's first appearance, distant growls and roars, trees toppling in the mid-distance, then his face . . . the destruction of the raft in the swamp lake, the great snake head rising out of the mists high above the bodies of the frightened men, dinosaurian jaws gaping grinningly, the head and neck gliding down into the water only to emerge under the raft and lift it into the air, the log-and-bamboo structure splitting and the men leaping for their lives . . . Kong taking off Fay Wray's clothes . . . Kong shaking the men off the log that spans the narrow chasm . . . Kong's fights with an assortment of primordial beasts . . . Kong's destruction of the Sixth Avenue elevated train in New York . . .

ESKIMO, 1933

◎◎◎◎◎◎◎◎◎◎◎◎◎◎◎◎◎◎◎◎◎◎◎

An early memory that still remains vivid is the scene in *Eskimo*, directed by W. S. Van Dyke, in which the native hero, Mala, handcuffed by a Mounted Policeman for a crime he didn't commit, works his wrists out of the cuffs by rotating them and pulling them through their steel loops during the course of a long night of oppression and suffering. He has worn all the skin away by the time he has achieved his freedom. He escapes and is pursued, but how it all ends I cannot remember.

LES MISERABLES, 1935

Les Miserables, based on the novel by Victor Hugo, is an epic, multi-year chase in which a relentless, law-by-the-book police inspector, Javert (played brilliantly by Charles Laughton), devotes his every waking moment toward the tracking down and apprehension of Jean Valjean (Fredric March, also at his best), who was sent by cruel French justice to the galley ships for stealing a piece of bread and who later escapes.

If this format seems at all familiar to younger readers, it is because they watched it a few years ago in a modern setting in the successful TV series "The Fugitive," in which David Janssen was the pursued and Barry Morse the dogged pursuer.

Set partly against the background of the French Revolution and told in a picaresque style, Les Miserables follows Jean Valjean through a number of adventures in which, time and again, the basic humanity and goodness of the man are revealed. But Javert is never far behind, and if Jean does not want to be returned to the galley ships, he must move on.

At film's end, our hero, having rescued actor John Beal from death and carried him through an endless maze of sewers (a splendidly visual sequence) beneath the riot-torn streets of Paris, is finally cornered by his nemesis. He asks for a few minutes to say goodbye to his family. As Javert waits outside Valjean's home, he watches his quarry through the window bid his last respects to his loved ones, and something curious begins to stir within him.

We cut to the interior of the house and Jean, in an extremely moving departure scene. Then he goes outside to face his destiny, resigned to the fact that he will be sent back to the galleys for the remainder of his days. But the street is empty. Javert has gone.

THE LIVES OF A BENGAL LANCER, 1935

⊙⊙⊙⊙⊙⊙⊙⊙⊙⊙⊙⊙⊙⊙⊙⊙⊙⊙⊙⊙⊙⊙⊙

In Henry Hathaway's *The Lives of a Bengal Lancer* there are two scenes that still send a ripple up my lumbar whenever I think of them and of that intensely memorable film of adventure.

In one the evil sultan, played by Douglas Dumbrille, tries to wrench some valuable information from Richard Cromwell by having burning bamboo splinters shoved under his fingernails. Hathaway doesn't actually let us see this ghastly business on screen, but he does let us see the reflection of the flaming sticks on the polished surface of a table top as they are advanced toward Cromwell's anchored hand.

Elsewhere in the film Franchot Tone sits reclined on a sofa playing his flute to the annoyance of his buddy, Gary Cooper, who, from an adjoining room, persistently but unsuccessfully tries to get him to stop. But then what should come along, gliding down from the rafters, but a cobra, which rears up from the floor a foot or so away from Tone's head and begins to weave back and forth as though it were under a snake charmer's spell. Tone can do nothing but play harder, louder, and faster. Eyes bugging from their sockets, his forehead lathered in sweat, he is too frightened to take his lips from the flute even for the second necessary to summon Cooper.

Tone's antics hit just the right comic note in counterpoint to the grimness of the situation. Cooper finally appears and gets his revenge on Tone by nonchalantly prolonging the suspense for a minute or so before calmly taking out his service revolver and blowing off the cobra's head.

THE BRIDE OF FRANKENSTEIN, 1935

Can you imagine the most horrifying of all screen monsters shedding a tear? Well, he did in *The Bride of Frankenstein*, a bizarre, freaky, kinky parody of the entire horror genre directed by one of Hollywood's most gifted and curious directors, James Whale. Whale was a Britisher with a dark-stained Gothic humor whose parodies were frequently designed to parody themselves. His talents were nowhere better displayed than in that scene in the blind hermit's hut where the monster, Boris Karloff, seeks refuge from pursuing villagers.

Termed a "pastoral grotesque interlude" by Carlos Clarens (he wrote *An Illustrated History of the Horror Film*), the scene permits the hermit to extend a deeply compassionate hospitality to his guest; he not only offers him the pleasures of his table and his cellar but plays a merry tune for him on his fiddle. Caught up in the warmth and humanity that has been bestowed upon him for the first time in his man-made existence, the Monster responds in kind. He emulates the old hermit by awkwardly accepting a cigar and sticking it into his mouth. He recoils at first from the lighted match that is offered him (he has a good memory, and for good reason) but finally permits his cigar end to be lit, and sits back in his chair, glass of wine in hand, puffing heavily but contentedly. His face beams in pleasure and good humor, and laughing, he says, "Smoke—*good!*" These are the first words uttered by the Monster.

Later, while being tucked into a cot amid shadows from the cheery fire that dance on the walls and ceiling of the cottage, he looks from his pillow position into the face of the blind man kneeling beside him and, in a moment of pure, miraculous irony, lets a large tear run down his cheek.

We are moved almost to tears ourselves, yet we want to laugh. We are reminded of Jackie Cooper being tucked into bed by Wallace Beery, yet we are watching the king of all monsters, an inhuman killer, in the presence of a kindly man who cannot see the face of his guest. We are watching a horror film and yet we are beholding a scene of compassion. We are, in short, catapulted into a mood of tragicomedy in a sequence of rococo wit that kids the pants off itself while it mocks all others of its kind.

We have hardly begun to exhaust the ironic levels of this episode, but we will leave it here before we demythologize it too completely. In one of the true works of cinematic imagination, Karloff's tear is an imperishable moment.

THE THIRTY-NINE STEPS, 1935

Alfred Hitchcock's *The Thirty-Nine Steps* simply bustles with notable screen moments. On the run across the moors of Scotland from police and spies alike, hero Robert Donat encounters a string of incidents that are pure vignettes in their suspense and mystery, their comedy, and their beautiful tailoring.

He blunders into a political meeting in a small town, is mistaken for the guest speaker, and delivers a nonsense speech with such style that he gains enthusiastic applause.

Caught on a street corner at night with his foes approaching from two opposite directions, there seems nowhere on earth that he can go. A Salvation Army band plus entourage comes marching by, and when Donat's enemies arrive at the corner where he was standing, he is no longer there. In a lovely track shot that follows the street band, the back of a head protrudes up from below the camera into the frame at extremely close range. Donat has joined the other marchers.

Earlier in the film Donat seeks refuge in the desolate moorland at the home of a local country squire. He has good reason to believe this man will help him by (a) granting him asylum and (b) giving him information as to the whereabouts and identity of the leader of the spy organization, a man identified only by the fact that the end of his little finger is missing. Godfrey Tearle plays the squire, and right away we share Donat's faith in the integrity of this man and the belief that he will help him. This sense of trust is borne out when police come to the door and Tearle sends them away on a ruse. But later, pouring a scotch and soda and extending the glass to our hero within the safe confines of his private study, Tearle reveals . . . the end of a little finger missing. Donat's eyes are worth everything here.

In another part of the film Donat becomes handcuffed to Madeleine Carroll and proceeds to drag her through a number of tense-funny episodes. The scene in the country inn where they must share a room for the night is particularly droll in light of prevailing mores and censorship codes of the day. At one point Carroll tries to take off her wet stockings, but as she puts down her hands to her legs Donat must bend down with her. His line "Can I be of any assistance?" drove audiences wild with delight.

And then there is the climax in a London music hall. Donat is sitting in the middle of a row, Godfrey Tearle is in an upper balcony box, and the Scotland Yard men are searching down both aisles, coming closer and closer. Finally they see Donat and start in toward him from both ends of the aisle. Donat rises, and with Madeleine Carroll goes toward the police to reason with them. But they intend to arrest him. They will not listen to his references to Godfrey Tearle or his explanations of how Mr. Memory, the great memory expert, who is on stage at that very moment, was assisting the spies in getting their secret formulas out of the country undetected. The moment is one of panic. There is now no way to turn, nothing Donat can do to avoid arrest. Up on the stage Mr. Memory is going through his nightly paces answering any questions put to him by his audience. And then, in a last desperate move, just as he is about to be seized by the police, Donat breaks away from them, rushes back toward the middle of his row, and in a loud, clear voice which I can still hear down through all the years calls to Mr. Memory, "What are the 'thirty-nine steps'?" Memory is momentarily stunned and seems to freeze in a terrible dilemma. "The thirty-nine steps?" he repeats. He pauses again, and in that brief interim we see the face of a man torn between his obligations to the spy ring and his loyalty to his stage profession. But thespianism wins out. "The 'thirty-nine steps' is an organization of spies whose leader—" is all he manages to get out. A bullet from an upper balcony, fired by the man missing the little finger, silences his voice.

44

THE SCARLET PIMPERNEL, 1935

It took a Leslie Howard to say it, and an Alexander Korda production to make it possible, but Howard's uttering of the word "England" in the last shot of *The Scarlet Pimpernel* is one of the great romantic moments in all filmdom.

In this final scene of the movie, directed by Harold Young, Howard is at the bow of his ship just before dawn, with Merle Oberon in his arms. During a long cat-and-mouse game set amid the turbulence of the French Revolution Howard, as the incredibly elusive "Pimpernel," has rescued many members of the nobility before Madame Guillotine could claim them, and has, by a clever trick, finally gained the upper hand over his adversary and pursuer, the wicked Chauvelin, played with teeth-grinding relentlessness by Raymond Massey. Now, his work done, he is escaping from France by ship across the English Channel.

Howard and Oberon gaze over an expanse of mist-shrouded water as the early morning light picks up the first gray traces of the coastline ahead. "England," he says, as they stand silhouetted against the ropes and sails and sky, and it is Everyman's evocation of homeland.

SAN FRANCISCO, 1936

W. S. Van Dyke's depiction of the famous earthquake in *San Francisco* has never been equaled in the mood of destruction created. Even 1975's *Earthquake* couldn't come near it despite a huge budget and much more screen time devoted to scenes of panic and chaos. The Van Dyke approach relied on some brilliant editing to achieve its results plus some very real special effects.

But there is one shot in this frenzied and awesome montage of collapsing masonry and crumbling statuary that lingers long in the memory. That is the moment in which a street splits apart into a long, narrow, yawning crevice, some citizens being propelled into it, others dangling desperately from its ragged asphalt and concrete edge. It is only a brief moment in a sequence of rapid-fire images—neither Clark Gable nor Jeanette MacDonald nor Spencer Tracy nor any of the supporting players are in it—but it is unforgettably stark.

MODERN TIMES, 1936

It is the Great Depression in a city somewhere in the U.S.A. A truck, carrying a long load of lumber with a red warning flag at the end of the load to alert other motorists, rounds a corner. This is a very normal, everyday event, as familiar to us today as it was forty years ago. But in the world of Charlie Chaplin, the everyday becomes the bizarre. The picture is *Modern Times* and the scene leads to one of the great laughs of the cinema. The red flag falls off the load. Chaplin, who happens to be sauntering casually along the street, picks it up and runs after the vehicle waving the flag to signal it to stop. In so doing, however, he causes a vast group of men who are unemployed and disgruntled and who interpret the event as the heralding of a workers' revolt to follow him. This shot of Chaplin racing down the street, waving his red flag and attracting an ever-swelling army of followers, the background score playing "Hallelujah, I'm a Bum," is pure gold.

DODSWORTH, 1936

⊚⊚⊚⊚⊚⊚⊚⊚⊚⊚⊚⊚⊚⊚⊚⊚⊚⊚⊚⊚⊚

Among film moments whose greatness is derived from the unconventional, the last shot of *Dodsworth* must rank with the most impressive.

Directed by William Wyler from a novel by Sinclair Lewis, the last scene has graceful camera movement, narrative surprise, performances by Walter Huston and Mary Astor (two of the screen's finest professionals), and a theme so rare in the land of the cinema that one sometimes forgets it possesses the universality that it does: middle-aged love. *Brief Encounter* is all about this neglected arena of delight, and Sidney Furie's brilliant, underrated film, *Hit*, contains at least one gorgeous example of it, but moviedom still hasn't pulled itself out of the harness of youth cult to become aware of it.

Walter Huston plays an American automotive manufacturer on his first holiday, with his wife, to Europe. She is talkative, *nouveau* upper middle crust, midwestern U.S.A. He is, well, just midwestern, warm, engaging, looking forward to enjoying this "first holiday in years."

As the story develops, Huston and his wife do different parts of Europe separately, and it is on his itinerary that Mary Astor, glimpsed briefly earlier in the film, comes prominently onto the scene. Huston and Astor fall in love, but Huston is true to his wife and will not let matters proceed to their natural conclusion. And so he leaves Mary Astor, with whom he is passionately in love, and returns to his wife. He does this because to him, it is the only honorable thing to do.

On board a large ocean liner, docked in a British seaport ready to sail, Huston and his wife are in a passenger salon saying goodbye to their European friends (mainly her friends). Huston has forgotten what an inane, vacuous, empty-headed chatterbox his wife really is. He realizes, sitting in the salon watching her and listening to her, that he is returning to a life of utter boredom simply because convention dictates it. He realizes that, after thirty years, he actually doesn't love his wife. He likes her, they have been partners, they have raised a family, but he doesn't really love her. And so we, the audience, expect a fade-out on the conventional type of semi-tragic, bittersweet ending we had been raised, by the Hays Office, to expect. But that ending doesn't materialize.

Instead, to our wide-eyed disbelief, Huston rises, looks at his wife long and solemnly and understandingly, and tells the porter to take his baggage ashore. His wife cannot comprehend. And neither can we, for a moment. Then Huston explains that he is leaving her and going to join someone else, that a continuation of their marriage would be both a serious mistake and a farce. She will be well looked after at home. She is well set, and she has her friends (hundreds of them). And so, before a gape-mouthed woman, he departs.

And then there is the last romantic shot: Huston standing upright in a motor launch approaching Mary Astor's villa in Italy, his fedora clutched in his hand, waving excitedly as he sees her on her veranda, and she waving back. The End.

THE HURRICANE, 1937

◎①◎◎◎◎◎◎◎◎◎◎◎◎◎◎◎◎◎◎◎◎◎◎◎

While John Ford's *The Hurricane* merits a citation for the sound track and visual effects created by James Basevi for the big storm at the climax, it is the way the denouement was handled that has particularly grabbed my memory.

Jon Hall as Tarangi, a native of a South Seas island under French control, is persecuted by the strict, unfeeling governor, played by Raymond Massey. Imprisoned on another island for a crime he didn't commit, Tarangi cannot stand the confinement and the subhuman treatment meted out by a sadistic guard, John Carradine, and so effects an escape by diving from an impossibly high cliff into the sea. He is recaptured but later feigns suicide and actually makes good his escape this time. He arrives home in time for the climactic storm, performs a number of acts of selfless heroism, and at film's close is rowing away with his wife, Dorothy Lamour, and wee baby toward another island and a new life.

On the beach amid the debris and destruction left in the wake of the holocaust, Mary Astor, wife of the governor, watches through a pair of binoculars Hall and his wife make their retreat. She is happy that they have escaped because, unlike her husband, she has grown to know something of the true worth and humanity of Tarangi. But her authoritarian, austere husband is standing only a short distance away and asks her what she is looking at through her glasses. Momentarily caught off guard, she replies it is only a piece of driftwood. Massey comes over to her, takes the glasses from her hands, puts them to his own eyes, and slowly brings them into focus. There, in the circular field of his vision, are Hall and Lamour and the baby. There is a long, incredibly pregnant pause, while Massey trains his glasses seaward and Astor waits. Finally, the governor puts down his binoculars and looks at his wife. "You are right," he says slowly. "Only driftwood." And so the film ends.

SABOTAGE, 1937

Sabotage does not come to mind as readily as, say, *The Thirty-Nine Steps* or *The Lady Vanishes* when one thinks of Hitchcock's great films, and the reason probably is the picture's over-all sordidness of tone plus one scene which is so utterly downbeat and harrowing that it tends to cast a pall over the entire picture.

Hitchcock afterward regretted having included this scene in the released version of the film, and from the standpoint of his popular reputation he was probably right. But from the standpoint of film art, this *scène noire* is an undoubted classic: grim, depressing, sadistic, negative, but brilliantly constructed, shot, and edited, and possessing a *shock* that we are led to anticipate but which we know, in all final humanity and sanity (and on the basis of traditional audience expectations), cannot possibly happen. Ahhhh, but it *does* happen, and it must be given its rightful place among the great screen moments.

Based upon Joseph Conrad's gloomy *The Secret Agent, Sabotage* recounts the tale of a group of anarchists who blow up public buildings. The London setting for most of the action is marvelous: an old house adjoining a small cinema where Sylvia Sidney, wife of sabotage specialist Oscar Homolka, lives and works. When not looking after the needs of her family, she tends to the ticket office of the movie theater, where the celluloid dreams that can be purchased for a few pennies form a counterpoint to the sordid reality of her life with Homolka.

The dark, disturbing scene occurs when Homolka sends Sylvia Sidney's young brother (about thirteen years old) on a bus to deliver a brown paper package to the Piccadilly Circus tube station. Unknown to the boy, but grimly known to the movie audience, is the time bomb that Homolka has implanted in the package. The boy, however, has a wide margin of time to execute his task, thus we are not immediately worried for his safety when the anarchist first sends him on his way. It is only when the laddie begins to encounter a few delays that our concern begins to mount. But then we tend to shrug off these presentiments when we realize Hitchcock isn't likely to blow up a small, thirteen-year-old boy.

The delays, alas, begin to increase: a sales demonstration that blocks the bus's progress, a long street parade of the Lord Mayor of London, and others. Traffic lights are a menace, and the crowds along the way become a restrictive horror as Hitchcock begins to cut from the boy in the bus window to nearby clocks, which reveal that the original margin of time has been consumed and that there is now every serious reason to believe the young man will be too late to reach his destination. Still, we silently say to ourselves, Hitchcock will never do this. The boy will be rescued; but how?

Now Hitchcock's camera, no longer satisfied with close-up cross-cuts from the boy's face to the moving second hand on giant clocks, cuts to interior shots of the brown paper package where the actual spring mechanisms of the time bomb become screen size. Swiftly we cut from the bomb's "hands" to the London street clock hands to the little boy's face to the passengers on the crowded bus to the brown package to the street crowds. Time is running out. The hour is almost at hand. Then in a terrifying explosion the bus and *all* its occupants are destroyed.

So much for the *scène noire*.

The climax is also vintage Hitchcock. Earlier, just after she had learned of the death of her little brother, Sylvia Sidney stabs the loathsome, brutish Homolka with a kitchen knife—actually she is holding it in front of herself for protection during an after-dinner row resulting from the tragic news, and he walks right into it. Subsequently she confesses to her boy friend, Scotland Yard man John Loder. Loder tries to convince her it was purely an accident, that there is no moral guilt upon her, and that she should *not* make any further confessions (to his "chief," for example) because there would probably be *no* way she could technically prove her innocence before a court of law. But Sylvia Sidney feels she cannot live with the memory of the death of her husband upon her mind.

As the police surround Homolka's house at the end and prepare to enter (the gang is there and this is roundup time), Sidney, who is outside on the street with Loder, approaches the Chief Inspector to tell all. He is standing on the curb beside his patrol car preparing to direct the final assault against the house. Homolka has not responded to his loudspeaker demands. Other members of the gang threaten to blow up themselves and the house if the police advance beyond the doorway. Sidney says to the Chief Inspector that she wants to tell him about her husband. He asks her what it is she wants to tell him. She responds, "He's dead."

At that precise moment there is a thundering explosion and the entire house goes up in smoke. The Scotland Yard men charge inside and report a few minutes later that "everyone" is dead. As the audience well knows, there is now no need for Sylvia Sidney to make any confession to the chief. The body of Homolka has been blown up along with all the other bodies. No knife wound could ever be detected.

As John Loder puts his arm around her and guides her off down the street . . . to freedom . . . the Chief Inspector gazes long and hard after the two of them, puzzled. "Funny," he says to an aide, "she said her husband was dead *before* the explosion went off." His gaze after the receding pair continues for what seems to be an interminable time. Then he says, "Or was it *after* the explosion?"

He shrugs, dismissing the entire issue, and turns to other business. Sidney and Loder continue their long walk as the movie comes to a close.

LOST HORIZON, 1937

⊚⊛⊛⊛⊛⊛⊛⊛⊛⊛⊛⊛⊛⊛⊛⊛⊛⊛⊛⊛⊛⊛

One of the great fantasy-romances of all time is Frank Capra's production of *Lost Horizon*, made from the novel by James Hilton. In this film Robert Conway, a British diplomat (Ronald Colman), finds Utopia in a lamasery in a remote Tibetan valley where water cascades over rocks and flows through glades into sunlit pools, where crops are harvested, where lamas pursue their studies in quaint library alcoves, and where people seem to age very slowly, while outside the valley, beyond the walls of granite, all is cold and snowy blizzard. This is Shangri-La, perfection incarnate, Everyman's dream, for Conway a lost world of exquisite peace and contentment. Here he has discovered Catherine (Jane Wyatt), a missionary's daughter, lovely and gracious, who teaches school for the Tibetan children in the valley, and he has fallen in love with her.

The moment in the film that ranks with the finest in moviedom occurs the night that John Howard as Conway's younger brother persuades Colman to leave Shangri-La. The High Lama (Sam Jaffe) who rules the valley has died and a long funeral procession bearing torches that flare eerily in the darkness moves in mournful lament around the great central pool of the lamasery. Conway, in trench coat and fedora, the chanting funeral column behind him, has moved up the long ascent to the cave entrance, which is the only means of access to the valley. There porters wait with clothing and supplies for the long journey across the mountains. Catherine has by now discovered that Conway is leaving and is running across the square calling his name, but he is too far up the slope to see or hear her. Conway's brother enters the cave tunnel that leads to the roaring snow beyond; Lo-Tsen (Margo) is with him, and the porters are nearby.

Before following, Robert Conway looks back toward his paradise, and although his brother is calling him impatiently, his eyes linger on the lamasery hugging the mountainside, on the ghostly flares, and on the dim outlines of the valley far below. Howard calls again and Colman's face almost turns away, but something magnetizes it and does not let it completely turn. This is the moment I have long remembered. Our hero realizes he may never find his Utopia again, may never see Catherine again (he admits he couldn't have left if he had had to say goodbye to her), but his loyalty to his brother is strong and he knows that without his leadership Howard would never be able to make it to the outside.

And so his face is held briefly in time as he lingers on the brink of a world that might soon be lost forever, but as the chanting soars up from below he pulls himself out of his reverie and passes into the cave.

Henry B. Walthall raises his sword to begin the famous charge in *The Birth of a Nation,* 1915.

Richard Barthelmess pursues Lillian Gish over the ice floes in *Way Down East,* 1920.

Jean Hersholt gets the edge on Gibson Gowland just before the fight to the death in *Greed*, 1924.
(Museum of Modern Art/Film Stills Archive)

Here's the face (Lon Chaney's) that Mary Philbin unveiled during the eerie mask-lifting sequence in *The Phantom of the Opera*, 1925.

This isn't my favorite moment from *Sunrise*, 1927, but it does show the protagonists, George O'Brien and Janet Gaynor, preparing for their fateful outing in the rowboat.

Chaplin buys a flower from Virginia Cherrill, the blind girl, early in *City Lights*, 1931.

A look at the satanic, almost loving presence and the crooked grin of Boris Karloff in *The Mask of Fu Manchu,* 1932.

King Kong prepares to shake his pursuers off a log into a treacherous
jungle canyon, 1933.

Douglas Dumbrille is about to administer burning bamboo splinters to
Gary Cooper's fingers in *The Lives of a Bengal Lancer,* 1935.

A cobra responds to Franchot Tone's flute playing and decides to keep him company while Gary Cooper stands by in *The Lives of a Bengal Lancer,* 1935.

The monster is consoled by the blind hermit just before the magic moment in *The Bride of Frankenstein,* 1935. ((Robert Scherl)

Madeleine Carroll is handcuffed to Robert Donat and must share a room with him for the night in *The Thirty-Nine Steps*, 1935.

Ronald Colman and party meet emissaries from Shangri-La following the plane crash in remote Tibet in *Lost Horizon*, 1937.

Ronald Colman duels with Douglas Fairbanks, Jr., in the exciting climax of *The Prisoner of Zenda*, 1937.

Naunton Wayne (left), Margaret Lockwood, Dame May Whitty, Michael Redgrave, Basil Radford, and Cecil Parker pose for a publicity photo for *The Lady Vanishes*, 1938.

THE PRISONER OF ZENDA, 1937

Whether exploring the wonders of a timeless valley in remote Tibet, or posing as the king of a mythical European country at a time of national strife, Ronald Colman *was* the great romantic of the motion picture screen. In *The Prisoner of Zenda*, David O. Selznick's masterwork of adventure and romance, there occurs a climactic duel between Colman (Rudolph Rassendyll the Third) and the film's dashing villain-adversary, Douglas Fairbanks, Jr. (Rupert of Hentzau), which has great panache and a unique final note.

At the conclusion of the long, beautifully choreographed sword fight up a great staircase to a room high in the castle, surprisingly, neither combatant kills the other. Fairbanks simply shakes his head, tosses his rapier into an oaken beam near Colman's head, leaps to the sill of an open window, and, laughing, says: "Goodbye, Englishman; we'll meet again!" Then he disappears in a long dive a hundred feet into the moat beneath. Colman watches him swim to the far side, where a waiting horse permits his escape. The bad man has gotten away, and properly so because of the spirit of mutual admiration which has built up between him and the hero during the film. And yet the idea of a villain escaping was wildly unconventional for the thirties.

Colman later rescues the imprisoned king (also played by Colman) and returns him to his bride, Madeleine Carroll. Then he makes his departure, saying goodbye to Carroll, whom he deeply adores and will never see again. C. Aubrey Smith (Colonel Zapp) and another close companion escort our hero by horse to the border, where, in a long hilltop shot, he waves farewell to his gallant friends and rides off for England and home.

Earlier, during the lavish coronation sequence in which Colman impersonates the king, there is a wide-angle, back-track shot of Colman and Carroll (who was unmatched in screen beauty in her day) coming toward us, arm in protocol arm, down an enormously broad staircase while the national anthem of Ruritania plays in the background. In sweep, opulence, grace, and dignity, there have been few shots like it.

ALI BABA GOES TO TOWN, 1937

⊙◎⊙◎⊙◎⊙◎⊙◎⊙◎⊙◎⊙◎⊙◎⊙◎⊙

Eddie Cantor plays a movie extra who falls asleep in a giant crock during the shooting of an Ali Baba flick. The picture is *Ali Baba Goes to Town* and in the film Cantor dreams he is the real Ali Baba undergoing a series of whimsical adventures in ancient Bagdad.

The wonderfully imaginative climax has our hero aboard a flying carpet soaring through the clouds, but the carpet somehow catches fire and, foot by foot, begins to burn. Finally there are only about two feet of carpet left, yet Cantor flies bravely, albeit nervously, onward. Then he has only one foot left! What a mad, mad sight! Turbaned Eddie Cantor roaring through the air on a one-foot carpet, smoke and flames trailing out the rear. And then there is hardly enough carpet to stand upon. Poor Eddie loses his balance and falls out of his dream.

ALEXANDER NEVSKY, 1938

⊚⊚⊚⊚⊚⊚⊚⊚⊚⊚⊚⊚⊚⊚⊚⊚⊚⊚⊚⊚⊚⊚

There is a battle in Sergei Eisenstein's *Alexander Nevsky* that lingers long in the memory, partly because of the swift editing of highly specific images, but mainly because of the unusual setting.

It is the thirteenth century. The battle is fought on a frozen lake and runs for about twenty minutes of screen time. The opposing forces are the Russian citizens of Pskov, with Nevsky as their leader, and the Teutonic Knights of Livonia, a province of Germany. Under Edward Tisse's camera and Eisenstein's cutting genius, the ice on the lake starts to break up as the battle nears its end and the German troops start to retreat. In an incredible panorama of detail ice floes come apart and capsize under the weight of fleeing bodies, letting them slip down through widening cracks into the black water below. Other knights grapple for support on cakes of ice but their armor is too heavy and they go under, their grim metal helmets with the dehumanized eyeslits turning over just beneath the surface of the water and facing skyward before disappearing.

The most telling shot, however, is where a cape is slowly pulled out of sight before our eyes down through a crack in the ice, obviously weighted by an unseen body below.

THE LADY VANISHES, 1938

Who can ever forget Dame May Whitty's face in the last shot of
The Lady Vanishes? May Whitty has long disappeared from the
screen, but that incredible image of her reaching up from the
keyboard of the piano directly into the camera—we are positioned between Margaret Lockwood and Michael Redgrave and
we are moving in with them, swiftly toward her—her arms outstretched lovingly toward friends who had been with her on a
desperate adventure and whom she might never have seen again,
this image captures so much human warmth, such devotion and
camaraderie, that one's emotions cannot be restrained.

By employing such an ending, Hitchcock gave a whole new
dimension to the suspense thriller and placed this picture in a
pantheon of favorites.

But this shot, like many great moments in the movies, while
pictorially evocative and well acted and maximizing audience
identity with the two heroes, Lockwood and Redgrave, does not
stand alone. For its complete appreciation, one has to have the
"whole cloth," as it were.

Briefly, Dame May Whitty is a British agent bound across
Europe for England by train with a secret message of grave military importance for her superiors. On the train she becomes
friendly with Margaret Lockwood, a young woman on vacation
from London. Later when Whitty mysteriously disappears and
Lockwood tries to find her, no one on the train will acknowledge
that she even existed. In fact they try to discredit Lockwood—
and slyly villainous Paul Lukas, playing a surgeon who is escort-
ing a patient on a stretcher to some distant terminal on the rail
line, is the chief offender here: he suggests that a bump she had

received earlier on her head has been causing hallucinations and that Dame May Whitty is a pure figment of her imagination.

Lockwood has even begun to doubt her own convictions when fellow passenger Michael Redgrave encounters evidence purely by accident to prove Lockwood correct. The label from a package of tea, an obscure brand but the very one Whitty is alleged to have carried in her purse, is blown up against a train window where it adheres for a few moments, long enough for Redgrave to see. It had been thrown out of the train with garbage by the porter moments before. Now begins the search in earnest with Lockwood and Redgrave pitted against Lukas and his aides.

Redgrave discovers Whitty wrapped from head to foot in gauze and lying on the hospital stretcher in Lukas' compartment (he had switched her with the "patient" he had brought on board earlier). But by this time all appears lost: the train has been driven over a border into Lukas' own national territory and ambushed in a remote wooded area. As Paul Lukas and his henchmen move in through the trees to regain custody of Miss Whitty, a gun battle with our friends on the marooned train ensues.

The situation grows extremely critical and Whitty makes a desperate decision. She hums several bars of music so that Redgrave can memorize them (the music carries the coded message for the British government) and makes him promise to take it to the military authorities in England for her. Then she slips through a window down the far side of the coach and runs across a field toward the border. Lukas fires at her retreating figure and we see her suddenly drop out of sight in the distance, whether by choice or as a result of the bullet we are not certain. Needless to say, Redgrave and team, through some delightful heroics, get the train moving again, this time in the direction of the border and safety. Lukas has lost his quest but gives his departing guests a good-natured wave as the train moves away and mutters, "Jolly good luck to them."

Now, back in London once more, Michael Redgrave suddenly suffers a lapse of memory and cannot remember the vital few bars of music Whitty had entrusted to him. There he stands beside Margaret Lockwood, in the foyer of a high government office in London, about to be taken into an inner office where key officials await his critical presence, and the whole message is lost. Defeat for Redgrave and girl friend Lockwood. But only momentarily.

Just as all appears thwarted, we hear the familiar strains of a tune drifting in from a piano off screen. Redgrave's face starts to brighten and he takes Margaret Lockwood's arm and begins to move through a door opening into the room from where the music originates. Hitchcock's camera takes a position between them and moves with them. And there ahead of us we see the source of the music. It is our wonderful British agent, Dame May Whitty. She is alive. She reaches up.

THE DAWN PATROL, 1938

⊚◎◎◎◎◎◎◎◎◎◎◎◎◎◎◎◎◎◎◎◎◎◎◎

Errol Flynn's "hedgehopping" in a double-winged Sopwith creates a scene of high adventure in *The Dawn Patrol*. But it is his farewell salute as he goes to his death that lingers long in the memory. It is a gesture representative of a vanished attitude toward war that for modern viewers is pure nostalgia. Flynn loses an aerial dogfight to a German airman whose ability he respects, and goes to his death. But he dies as no one ever dies any more in movies, a romantic exit that owes more to Queen Victoria than General MacArthur. His plane aflame, blood oozing from the corner of his mouth, he salutes his victor with his gloved hand and, a tragic grin on his moustached face, rolls slowly off screen to his oblivion.

SWISS MISS, 1938

@@@@@@@@@@@@@@@@@@@@@@@@@

In *Swiss Miss* Laurel and Hardy achieved one of their pinnacle moments in screen comedy. The moment is a split one. In the first part we see Laurel and Hardy attempting to move a piano across a rope bridge that spans a Swiss gorge. They are at one end of the piano, and a gorilla is at the other end. The antics are hilarious, the upshot being the fall of the gorilla over the side of the bridge into the chasm below. Now jump to the very end of the film. Laurel and Hardy have completed their adventures in Switzerland and are coming out onto a mountain road to head home. As they march merrily away the camera pans over to a clump of bushes and there, lo and behold, stands the very gorilla they had "taken care of" earlier in the picture, only he has a bandage around his head and is maneuvering on crutches. The vengeful gorilla hobbles out into the middle of the road glaring venomously at the departing pair. Laurel turns for some reason, sees the ape, and starts to break into one of his tremendous mime-hysterias in which he visually weeps while pointing in a frenzied state at the focus of his attention. Hardy now sees who is confronting them. Holding onto his bowler hat he grabs Stanley's arm and the pair run off down the road as fast as they can. The gorilla calmly watches their bodies recede into the distance; then, when they are no more than two "specks" on the horizon, the gorilla takes one of his crutches and begins to swing it round and round over his head. He lets go and sends the projectile veering off toward the pair of "dots" on the distant horizon. He waits for a few seconds watching patiently. The two "dots" fall over.

THE HOUND
OF THE BASKERVILLES, 1939

◎◈◈◈◈◈◈◈◈◈◈◈◈◈◈◈◈◈◈◈◈◈◎

In the last shot of Sidney Lanfield's film version of *The Hound of the Baskervilles* Basil Rathbone as Sherlock Holmes utters what must be one of the great tragic lines of all mysterydom. Deeply fatigued, and overcome by an enormous letdown following the death of the "beast" and the solution of the strange mystery on the Devonshire moors, Holmes turns at the bottom of a staircase and says to his faithful friend and foil: "The needle, Watson." Ironically, back in 1939 the line was regarded more lightly than today because there was little drug consciousness. Nowadays the line produces an even greater tragic shudder.

GUNGA DIN, 1939

Gunga Din belongs to a special genre of films which, while cele-
brating the glories of the British Empire, owed more to the rug-
ged spirit of bold men, fair ladies, high adventure, and noble
purpose than to any particular imperialistic credo. Such motion
pictures were really "landed swashbucklers" inasmuch as vast
battles, extravagant derring-do, personal heroism, devotion, self-
sacrifice, honor, male camaraderie, and idealized love of woman-
kind were their hallmark, no different here than in *Captain
Blood*, *The Sea Hawk*, and many others. *Gunga Din* joins *The
Lives of a Bengal Lancer*, *The Charge of the Light Brigade*,
Drums, *Four Feathers*, and, not to neglect the finest of them all,
The Adventures of Robin Hood as pure adventure-entertain-
ment. Because of the special panache brought to it by George
Stevens it remains one of the very best of its genre. We could
well add to this list any number of Westerns, particularly the
breed in which Errol Flynn usually starred—*They Died with
Their Boots On* was the best—because they too followed the
same adventure-spectacle code. And, when dealing with the Indians, the same philosophy of imperialism, I might add. The fact
remains that while the British Empire is no more and imperialism, overt imperialism, that is, is no longer in favor, pictures
like *Gunga Din* and *The Lives of a Bengal Lancer* are still as
fresh and vibrant as ever, because they were well made and
were damned entertaining.

In *Gunga Din* Cary Grant, Victor McLaglen, and Douglas
Fairbanks, Jr., have the time of their lives trying to put down a
fanatical murder cult led by Eduardo Ciannelli as the Kali, but it

is Sam Jaffe as the thin, bent, tireless, loyal water boy of the title, who wants so desperately to be a bugler, who steals the show.

The moment that will always stand out in my mind occurs at the end when the British troops are about to be ambushed as they approach the entrance of the traditional pass (has there ever been another setting for the climax of a Hollywood film laid in India during Britain's occupation?). Our intrepid heroes had been captured earlier by the Kali and are being held in a temple with Sam Jaffe, who has sustained a fatal bullet wound. But Gunga Din will not say die, not yet at any rate. Marshaling a last gasp of strength and courage, he climbs to the top of a tower where a long, clear blow from his bugle will still be able to warn the British in time for them to take proper cover before becoming entrapped in the narrow defile below.

Atop the tower Gunga Din has his fleeting moment of glory, but as he is finishing his clarion call, a second bullet cuts him clean through the heart. Din's body slumps forward while his lips blow their last, and it is this "final" sound that comes from the bugle that I shall never forget. Instead of having Jaffe end on a clear, high note before sliding from the tower to his death, Stevens has him play out his final notes in a fading, non-musical rasp, perfect in its realistic, counterpointing effect. The awkward, dying note says it all.

STAGECOACH, 1939

⊚⊙⊚⊙⊚⊙⊚⊙⊚⊙⊚⊙⊚⊙⊚⊙⊚⊙⊚⊙⊚⊙⊚

The most graphic, rip-snortingest chase ever presented on the screen takes place in *Stagecoach*, John Ford's Western masterpiece. Across vast salt flats, a stageload of oddly assorted characters is being pursued by a band of hooting, hollering, savage, murderous Indians who, by a whole series of grimly connected incidents extending the length of the picture and building to this climax, are clearly bent on removing every white man from the face of their land. The drivers are killed or wounded and the reins are lost; John Wayne makes his famous leap out among the team of charging horses so that he can clamber to the front and mount the leader. Arrows rip through the coach and imperil John Carradine, Thomas Mitchell, Donald Meek, and the others. Hundreds of rounds of ammunition are fired and Indian after Indian bites the dust. Finally, when all appears lost, bugles sound faintly in the far distance and, as we grow increasingly aware of them, Ford cuts to a great moving camera shot of the American cavalry riding to the rescue.

The picture may have been short on enlightened sociology and may have, therefore, neglected to tell us how justifiably motivated the Indians were, but who could have expected more in 1939? The fact remains that, as a Western chase, this scene thunders head and tail over them all.

The Forties

Just as a star in outer space enters a supernova stage and achieves a maximum effulgence and iridescence on the very eve of its plunge to death, so the motion picture industry in the mid-forties gained a productivity it had never known before and immediately began to fall into sharp decline. In 1946 its gross income had grown to nearly 2 billion dollars; by the end of the decade it had dropped by 400 million dollars and had fallen into a depression from which it would never fully recover.

If the thirties may be seen as representing the growth and establishment of the studio factory system, the forties may be characterized as the canonization of that system. The gradual marriage of the means of production and exhibition accounted for this. But when in 1945 eight major companies were taken to court on charges of monopoly relating to this kind of multiple ownership, a death knell was clearly beginning to toll.

In addition to this, rising costs in production, the witch-hunting hysteria of the House Committee on Un-American Activities, the failure to recapture certain prewar markets, the high taxes imposed on the Hollywood product by other overseas markets, and the coming of television—these factors may offer some explanation for the decline in profit.

The mid-forties saw the giant studio monoliths at the peak of their power, profits, and professionalism. The star system, nurtured for thirty years, provided us with the most glittering array of gods and goddesses we have ever worshiped. Bogart, Bergman, Davis, Crawford, Cooper, Gable, Flynn, Cagney, Grable, Faye, Romero, Cummings, Sheridan, Russell, Reagan, Tracy, Turner, Rooney, Garland, Sinatra, Kelly, Stanwyck, Bacall, Ladd, Milland, Lake, Goddard, Hayworth, Ford, Power, Fonda, Tierney, Wayne, Crosby, Baxter, Montez, Hall, Sabu, Hutton, Astaire—these are some examples.

And directors like Welles, Hawks, Ford, Sturges, Hitchcock, Lang, Wilder, Capra, Wyler, Chaplin, Minnelli, Lubitsch, Cukor, and Wellman created some of their finest pictures, as did such writers as Herman Mankiewicz, Robert Riskin, Lamar Trotti, Nunnally Johnson, Robert Sherwood, I. A. L. Diamond, Ben Hecht, Philip Dunne, and many, many others.

Overseas, Britain was experiencing, in the immediate postwar period, its greatest time of productive creativity. *Dead of Night*, 1945, a masterpiece of the uncanny, was made by Cavalcanti and several other directors; *Brief Encounter, Great Expectations,* and *Oliver Twist* were all made by David Lean from '46 to '49; Pressburger and Powell led with *I Know Where I'm Going* (1945), *Stairway to Heaven* (1946), *Black Narcissus* (1946), and *The Red Shoes* (1948); Alexander Mackendrick directed *Tight Little Island* (1948); and Carol Reed made *Odd Man Out* (1946), *The Fallen Idol* (1948), and *The Third Man* (1949).

On the American front it was perhaps ironical that at a time when movie moguls like Louis B. Mayer, Darryl Zanuck, Adolph Zukor, the Warner Brothers, Sam Goldwyn, Harry Cohn, and David O. Selznick exerted such a tight, tough control over their factory empires and, in the instance of Goldwyn and Selznick, their independent production empires, some of the finest motion pictures we have ever seen were made.

This, the peak decade in the history of motion pictures, belongs to them.

THE GREAT DICTATOR, 1940

In *The Great Dictator* Charlie Chaplin creates a sequence of remarkable impact which is a delicate amalgam of concept and stagecraft. The greatest of film moments, it would seem, are intensely complicated in idea and cinematic structure and visual display, and yet their ironic genius is that they seem to come off so simply, so smoothly, so effortlessly. Mind you, they have to come off simply in the movies because the movies are a popular art form. The movies are the antithesis of elitism. They have never lost their original birthright of circuses and back streets and shabby halls. It is for this reason that directors like Chaplin and Hitchcock and Sturges have succeeded so brilliantly. Their materials were always up to far more than appeared on the surface, and yet on their "appearance" level they could be quickly and effortlessly grasped by the millions who came to see them.

Genius in the movies is hamburger prepared by a French chef.

When Chaplin was making *The Great Dictator*, there was a storm of protest over the idea of producing fun out of Hitler. When *The Great Dictator* was released, it was realized that Chaplin had created a monumental diatribe against the Führer, and yet he had accomplished his feat with the tools he knew best: slapstick, farce, satire, irony.

My favorite scene takes place when Chaplin as Herr Hynkel does a ballet in his imperial office with a large, balloon-like globe of the world. He holds the world delicately between outstretched hands and stares down at it with a sense of fatherly possession and the desire to care for and look after. For a moment we are almost beguiled by the dedication on his face, but then in a flash we realize it is the *entire world* he wants to care

73

for and *look after*. Dictatorship and totalitarianism blend into our view without Chaplin ever changing his expression. Then, insanity of insanities, Chaplin (attired in his Hitler uniform throughout all this, I might add) raises the balloon aloft and lets it spin on the ends of the fingers of one hand. Megalomania sweeps into the screen, sick, mad, maniacal megalomania. After this turn, Chaplin sends the world floating up to his high ceiling, and when it comes drifting gently downward, he stands, turned slightly at an angle away from the descending globe with the fingers of both his hands interlaced almost girlishly below his waistline, and gives it a light rear kick with his heel. Up it goes and down it comes for a repeat of this action. Then Chaplin bounces it upward with his head. Finally, he lies down on his desk and, as the *pièce de résistance*, when the balloon comes floating down to him, gives it an upward bounce with his fanny. This really says it all. This is Chaplin's message about Hitler.

After a repeat of this gesture, Chaplin leaps up on top of his desk and catches the descending globe with great adoration in both arms. He then jumps to the floor of his office and assumes a very stylized profile posture, military, firm, determined, as he gazes at the world that has grown up under his care, and that he has been making ballet love to, and has seduced, and conquered. At least he looks as though he has conquered it. It is at this moment that another dash of inspired genius occurs. Boom! the world blows up in front of him. And all that he has left is spittle all over his face and a wet, tattered rag of rubber sticking to the fingers of one hand. He bursts into tears, whirls away from us, and, his back to the audience, puts his head down on his desk and weeps hysterically.

NIGHT TRAIN TO MUNICH, 1940

Rex Harrison is trapped high over a gorge on the German-Swiss border in a cable car being hauled back toward the German side by Paul Henreid in Carol Reed's *Night Train to Munich*. Henreid, an officer in the Nazi military, has jammed the forward gears of the cable machinery with his rifle so that even if someone broke into the cable control room in which he has stationed himself in an attempt to send Harrison winging safely on his way back toward Switzerland, he would be powerless to reverse direction.

Resigned to his doom Harrison stares blankly from the window of his car toward the approaching tower where Henreid, revolver in hand, waits to capture him. And then, at the darkest moment, a ray of hope.

Coming out from the German side to pass him at mid-point over the abyss between the two countries is the companion cable car. If Harrison can make the leap to the car heading in the opposite direction, he will be safe.

With no time to lose he climbs through the window of his car and clings precariously to the door. The other car comes closer and closer. It will pass about ten feet away from him, an inconceivable distance for him to jump from a still position. But jump he does and, what's more, he makes it. The leap is grand and romantic and promptly puts the picture into the land of legend. Unable to alter the controls, his quarry receding in the distance toward Switzerland, Henreid shrugs, grins in grudging respect, holsters his gun, and walks away. Harrison sweeps into the waiting arms of Margaret Lockwood as his cable car docks on the far side and the film ends.

THE THIEF OF BAGDAD, 1940

Sabu takes a magic carpet ride in *The Thief of Bagdad,* produced by Alexander Korda, that ranks among the finest illusions ever created for the screen.

In one breathtaking flight of fancy the carpet glides along a main street in ancient Bagdad scarcely inches above the heads of the crowd. We see the carpet from a good distance, which only serves to heighten the magic because there is nowhere in evidence any visible means of support. When Sabu spies Prince Ahmed (John Justin) on a platform kneeling before a block with his head bent over it awaiting death, he takes aim with his bow and fires an arrow into the back of the executioner just as the upraised ax in the man's hands is about to descend. Then the great moment occurs.

Justin escapes from his guards and leaps from the scaffolding, landing on the moving carpet beside Sabu, who stands bravely, bow at the ready, awaiting his next peril. The thing that got me as a teen-ager when I first saw this scene was the fact that Justin's feet actually sank into the carpet when he made his leap, thus removing any thoughts from viewers about a board being used to keep the carpet in its flattened, horizontal pose. This was verisimilitude, and extremely effective.

Moments later, Sabu and Justin sweep off after villain Conrad Veidt, gliding up the face of the castle wall and over the turrets just in time to discover Veidt galloping from the roof on a mechanical horse, a horse, incidentally, which has just been wound up by an enormous key. As Veidt circles in the sky overhead, Sabu screams his name, "Jaffar!!" Veidt turns and looks downward, the handsome villainy of his moustached face and black-turbaned head never more possessive of screen presence than at this moment. Then Sabu once more takes aim with his dreadful bow, and an "arrow of truth" embeds itself in the middle of the wicked vizier's forehead. Veidt falls to his death and the flying horse disintegrates into a shower of springs, wheels, legs, flanks, and divers other mechanisms.

But this is not the only miracle in what is perhaps the greatest fantasy-adventure film ever made. Earlier, Sabu comes upon a bottle on a lonely beach, a bottle that contains the impish form of a genie (Rex Ingram) who converts to monstrous billows of smoke when Sabu opens the stopper and lets him out, only to condense, amid gales of thunderous laughter, into a two-hundred-foot version of his former diminutive self. After a bout or two of clever trickery during which our young hero gains the promise of "three wishes" from the genie, Sabu commands the creature to take him to the temple of the "all-seeing eye," where he hopes to secure a magic crystal ball that will permit him to locate the whereabouts of the prince (John Justin). The genie places Sabu (who is now very small in comparison) on his shoulder at the back of his neck where he can cling onto the genie's hair, and then, in another of those wonderful moments of supreme imagination, runs along the beach and, arms outstretched, proceeds to take flight. That was the moment!—where Ingram's body takes off from the sand. Superb.

Then we fly with the genie and his tiny passenger "halfway round the world." These shots, most of them filmed with the back of Ingram's head and outstretched arms in the immediate foreground and vast mountainous terrain below, contain a swelling symphony chorale on the sound track and combine to create one of the most romantic montages ever produced on the silver screen.

Finally, there is the scene in which the genie gains his freedom. Sabu has scaled the interior of the temple with the all-seeing eye, has successfully dispatched one or two giant spiders, and now has the magic jewel safely in his possession. The genie has granted the young thief his three wishes, has kept his bargain, and is now under no further obligation to serve him. When Sabu requests an additional wish—he has seen John Justin's image in the crystal ball and now wants to travel swiftly to him to save him from imminent execution—the gigantic Rex Ingram responds, "I am sorry, young master of the universe, but I have already granted you your three wishes. I have waited two thousand years for this moment. Now I am free!" Whereupon he sprints to the edge of a great canyon, looks back briefly, says farewell to his friend, then leaps into the yawning abyss, arms outstretched, and swoops away like a bird yelling, ". . . free . . . free . . . free . . ."

THE GREAT McGINTY, 1940

The most moving of all famous movie phone call sequences occurs in *The Great McGinty,* produced, written, and directed by Preston Sturges. The film is a brilliant satiric comedy, and the first of a series of highly personalized and very American gems by this remarkable motion picture maker. It details the rise, back in the thirties, of a bum to the status of state governor. Brian Donlevy plays the bum and Akim Tamiroff portrays his "boss," an unscrupulous politician who helps him reach the top and who stays around to "collect" through shady construction deals, etc., even when Donlevy tries to shake him off.

Imprisoned for fraud, Donlevy and Tamiroff escape and set out for asylum in South America, but before leaving the country Donlevy makes a farewell call from a telephone booth to his wife.

It is night, it is raining. Tamiroff, standing by their car, is impatient. Donlevy, in his East Side vernacular, explains to his wife that he must go away for a while. As he tells her where to find the key to their safe-deposit box, describes the contents which are more than enough to look after her, and tells her to watch out for their son, he is compressing a lifetime of love and devotion into the space of a few minutes and into simple language that never stoops to false sentiment and so becomes powerfully moving.

The film ends as it begins, in a saloon somewhere in the South American wilds. An argument between Donlevy and Tamiroff erupts into a fist fight, a course of action repeated a dozen times throughout the film, and bartender (and long-time crony to the pair) William Demarest looks directly into the camera and says, "Here we go again, folks!"

FANTASIA, 1940

⊚◎◎◎◎◎◎◎◎◎◎◎◎◎◎◎◎◎◎◎◎◎

"The Sorcerer's Apprentice" sequence in Disney's full-length *Fantasia* may be the most nightmarish sequence in cartoon fantasyland ever animated. And all the more effective because its star performer, Mickey Mouse, is featured in a role quite different from his short film appearances that audiences had grown used to for some thirteen years up to that time (*Plane Crazy*, circa 1927, was his first appearance, followed by *Gallopin' Gaucho* and the famous *Steamboat Willie* in 1928). With music derived from a scherzo for orchestra by Paul Dukas and conducted by Stokowski, the opening segment of this single episode has Mickey toiling for his master, an old wizard, by endlessly sweeping his master's abode and continually carrying water in wooden buckets to assist the magician's incantations, and there is much fun and humor here.

Then Mickey dons the fez and wand and tries to create some magic himself. Lo and behold the apprentice discovers he *does* possess some powers of sorcery because before one can say "abracadabra" he has the broom doing all the sweeping and water-carrying, leaving himself plenty of time to loaf and idle. But the magic soon gets out of control, and Mickey discovers he does not have the power to bring his magic to an end. The broom divides into two brooms to bring twice the water up to the sorcerer's stone container, then into four, eight, sixteen brooms. Soon hundreds of brooms are marching in endlessly insane processions carrying and pouring out hundreds of buckets of water into the container, which overflows in a great deluge that engulfs Mickey in tidal-wave proportions. But the marching brooms do not cease. They continue to multiply and carry water up the stone steps and down into the abode, even marching through the sea they have created in their determined task to pour water into the sorcerer's well. The scherzo score, the awesome number of spooky brooms accompanied by their infinite and eerie shadows, the terror registered on Mickey's face, the wild motion and the rapid cutting, the genius of the full animation system used with its remarkable color compositions, these combine to build the scene into the finest example of the animated cartoon since *Gertie the Dinosaur* first flicked across a screen in 1909.

THE MARK OF ZORRO, 1940

◉◎◉◎◉◎◉◎◉◎◉◎◉◎◉◎◉◎◉◎◉◎◉

Tyrone Power faces Basil Rathbone in the climactic duel of *The Mark of Zorro*, directed by Rouben Mamoulian. Before squaring off against each other, Rathbone intends to gain an initial psychological advantage over his opponent by grinningly going over to a burning candle and, with a sudden sharp sweep, shearing off the flaming top an inch below its wick.

Not to be outdone, Power approaches another burning candle and makes an almost identical sweep with his sword. But nothing happens. The candle continues to burn. Rathbone roars with laughter at the obvious "miss." Then, very calmly, Power reaches over and lifts the top off the candle. Rathbone glares incredulously.

FOREIGN CORRESPONDENT, 1940

⊚⊚⊚⊚⊚⊚⊚⊚⊚⊚⊚⊚⊚⊚⊚⊚⊚⊚⊚⊚⊚⊚

I have often thought *Foreign Correspondent* to be the quintes-
sential Hitchcock. Lacking, perhaps, some of the precise control
and sequential shaping of *The Lady Vanishes* or *The Thirty-
Nine Steps* (Hitchcock's two finest films), *Foreign Correspondent* is not his best picture but it does blend a first-rate plot
of international intrigue and mystery with expert character
sketches and comes up with the right balance of scenes, all totally cinematic, that combine to produce the magic for which he
is famous. Here are a few examples, all of them high moments in
the history of the cinema:

(1) The assassination sequence is done with marvelous panache in a rainstorm on the crowded steps of a government building in what seems to be Amsterdam. All we can see is a sea of
black umbrellas. So when Albert Basserman is shot by the fake
photographer as he is coming down the steps, we follow the assassin's retreat through the crowds as we would a ripple on a
pond, albeit an erratic ripple, for all we can detect is a line of
disturbance running through the vast panoply of umbrellas. We
never catch a glimpse of what is causing this disturbance from
beneath.

(2) Walking across a Dutch lowland, hero Joel McCrea encounters a windmill with its sails turning in a direction opposite
to that in which the wind is blowing. This operation turns out to
be a signal to an encircling plane and leads McCrea from one
peril to another, but the visual effect of the great structure rotating in this odd fashion, everything absolutely flat around it for
miles, the only sound being the soughing of the wind, is quite
riveting.

(3) George Sanders' escape from the clutches of spies who are attempting to torture information out of him is real bravura fare. He leaps through the plate-glass window of a hotel room three or four stories above a crowded street. His body drops straight downward, hits an arcade-like awning which breaks the fall, his hands grasping one of the awning's iron rods which is used to further break the fall as his body rips through the canvas sheeting and swings to the pavement.

(4) Gentle, amiable Edmund Gwenn is engaged by spymaster Herbert Marshall as an assassin to "do in" the nosy newspaper correspondent, and he proceeds to consummate his grisly task as a London guide in a tall observation tower (an anachronism, really, in the unskyscrapered London of those years, but acceptable in Hitchcockland). Watching Gwenn working to keep McCrea's attention focused on the "view" while coping with such annoyances as other tourists who simply do not understand that the tower must be emptied of all observers before a proper murder can be executed is a frustrating joy. These occupational hazards faced by Gwenn are handled with such superb "irritation" that Hitchcock actually manages to redirect our sympathies from McCrea to his Cockney guide for a fleeting moment or two. And then, just when all is clear, there is that "final" couple who stroll into view, the girl wanting to walk down to the street by the stairs, the man wanting to wait for the elevator. A shrewd, polite intercession by Gwenn, favoring the opinion of the girl, and the couple are off toward the stair entrance. And now the tower is dead empty. McCrea is just about to turn away from his observation perch for the fifth time in order to tell his guide he has really seen quite enough and wants to return to the street when Gwenn slowly, ever so slowly, backs away from McCrea about six paces, all the while chatting to him helpfully about where the Horse Guards are in his field of vision (McCrea looking and looking but failing to spot them). Then, a look of sinister violence on his face, hands outstretched in front of him in a "push" attitude, Gwenn charges right at us, directly into the screen.

Cut to two pedestrians on the street below looking up at the tower, the woman screaming in horror. Cut to a shot of someone falling from the structure all the way to the pavement beneath.

Cut to children running to see what has happened, leaving two nuns crossing themselves. Guess who fell?

(5) Finally, there is the scene in which the airliner our heroes are taking to get back to New York (war has just broken out) crashes into the Atlantic. Hitchcock actually stages the event in a brilliant single shot technique from the vantage point of the flight deck and does not cut to the usually obligatory "side view" showing the plane (a model) crash. Under Hitchcock's hands, we the audience are positioned directly behind the two pilots watching the water come closer and closer through the windscreen. When the actual crash occurs, we do not budge. Water bursts through the window ahead of us, pours over the control panels, engulfs the two pilots, and roars and fumes right into the camera.

THE RETURN OF FRANK JAMES, 1940

⊚⊚⊚⊚⊚⊚⊚⊚⊚⊚⊚⊚⊚⊚⊚⊚⊚⊚⊚⊚⊚⊚

There is a nice poetic touch at the end of Fritz Lang's *The Return of Frank James* that mixes reality with nostalgia and rounds off the story content with a flourish.

Frank James, played by Henry Fonda with a wad of tobacco in his mouth (a carry-over from *Jesse James* [1939], but certainly unusual for a hero in films), has succeeded in tracking down the murderers of brother Jesse. He is on the main street of the town where much of the action takes place and he is saying goodbye to Gene Tierney. He really wants to ask her to marry him, but he is kind of awkward and slow and never gets the proper words out. And she would like him to ask her (they have been through so much together) but custom prevents her from making the overture and, besides, she can't wait forever. And so they part, each going separate ways, she giving him a little wave of her hand before disappearing from view. The camera then closes in on a board wall where an ancient, half-torn poster bears the legend: "Jesse James, Wanted Dead or Alive, $5000 Reward." A wind rises, rips at the poster, and tears it away.

MAN HUNT, 1941

Man Hunt, directed by Fritz Lang, was based upon Geoffrey
Household's novel *Rogue Male,* and like its literary precursor
was an enormously successful cat-and-mouse thriller with strong
suspense-adventure appeal. It starred Walter Pidgeon as the
Englishman, Thorndyke; George Sanders as the Nazi Kuive-
Smith; Joan Bennett as Kitty, the Cockney streetwalker who be-
friends Thorndyke; and John Carradine as the sinister Mr. Jones.

The tale begins just before the outbreak of World War II. An
eerie opening shows Thorndyke, a famous big-game hunter,
lying astride a rocky outcropping overlooking Berchtesgaden and
speculating upon the possibilities of actually taking aim with his
telescopic rifle on Adolf Hitler's figure, which is moving back
and forth behind a large window several hundred feet below. He
levels his rifle carefully, the dictator's back directly in its sights,
but the gun only "clicks" when he presses the trigger.

"It would be that simple," his face registers, as he looks up
from his barrel. He thinks for a moment, ponders, and his eyes
grow quizzical. Then, almost fancifully, he inserts a shell in the
breech, lies prone, and reaims his barrel toward Hitler. His
finger caresses the trigger, but he never has the opportunity of
finding out whether he really wants to assassinate the German
leader or not because at that precise moment two Nazi guards
jump him and haul him before the interrogation specialist,
George Sanders.

As matters soon develop Sanders wants Pidgeon to sign a confession admitting (falsely, of course) that he had been sent by
Britain to kill Hitler. Sanders would use this confession to stir up
an international scene, strategically needed by Germany at that

point in its history. But Pidgeon escapes and, pursued by Sanders, Carradine, and a swarm of relentless Nazi agents across Europe and the U.K., finally seeks refuge in a cave in remote northern England, which is where the climax occurs.

With a cot and a few simple provisions procured from a village store a few miles away, Pidgeon has set up a kind of temporary domicile, primitive but efficient, and it is here he hopes to bide time until the Nazis give up their chase. But George Sanders is not to be eluded, and one afternoon turns up on the site. Pidgeon is now cast in the role of so many animals he has hunted all his life, trapped in a hole with only one exit, death. Sanders, in some gorgeously sinister underplaying, tells Pidgeon that all he wants is his signature on a note acknowledging he has been commissioned by the British Crown to kill der Führer, and that if he will sign he can go free. But Pidgeon knows that Sanders will never let him get away alive.

Pidgeon is a resourceful man—after all, he has spent much of his life in the wilderness—and when Sanders extends to him, through a narrow air hole, a stick with a little silver arrow on the end of it to which is attached the note he is supposed to sign, his mind grasps the first glimmerings of the modus operandi for his survival. But not before the full emotional significance of the pin has crashed upon him: it was a gift Pidgeon had given a Cockney woman (Joan Bennett) who had befriended him during some desperate hours in London scant days before. Its presence on the stick is clear: she has been killed by the villains. Sanders, from his position seated on a rock immediately outside the air hole, quietly comments that the girl had fallen accidentally from her window. Hearing Sanders, Thorndyke's mind craving revenge, his eyes riveted upon the silver arrow, the full plan for his escape goes into motion.

First, to stall Sanders, he tells him he has decided to sign the letter accepting guilt for the attempt on Hitler's life. Then, within the span of a few feverish minutes, he does several things. With one of his hiking boot laces he binds the silver arrow to one end of the stick and then uses his knife to notch the other end. Next he pulls out one of the wooden slats from his crude cot and quickly tapers and notches both of its ends. Then he undoes his other boot lace and proceeds to tie it like a cord to both ends of his tapered wooden slat. Suddenly we see his instrument for what it is: a crude but acceptable bow.

In the classic moment this sequence has been building toward, Thorndyke tells Kuive-Smith to roll the stone away, that he is coming out. Sanders does so, standing just to one side of the entrance, gun in hand, waiting for Pidgeon to emerge. Sanders' head is now in perfect profile beyond the air hole. Satisfied with the perspective of his target, Thorndyke puts his bow over the hole, places both feet firmly upon its shaft, inserts the notched end of the arrow into the cord so that its silver tip is pointed into the hole toward its objective, then proceeds to draw back the cord with both hands to the extremity of its tension.

Then he fires.

The arrow goes right through Sanders' head.

Like the novel the film ends with Thorndyke bailing out of a Wellington bomber somewhere over Germany, a telescopic rifle strapped to his back, an off-screen voice stating that he was resuming pursuit of his quarry and that this time he would not miss.

HOW GREEN WAS MY VALLEY, 1941

⊙⊛⊛⊛⊛⊛⊛⊛⊛⊛⊛⊛⊛⊛⊛⊛⊛⊛⊛⊛⊛⊙

At the end of John Ford's epic romance of the Welsh coal mines, *How Green Was My Valley*, when the father, Donald Crisp, is killed in a mine disaster and his body is brought up by cage to the surface, his head cradled in the arms of his young son, Roddy McDowall, the entire film proceeds to sweep into a reprise of some of its key scenes.

We see Walter Pidgeon as Reverend Griffyd walking along the beautiful valley before the slag heaps had begun to crawl down its slopes, Maureen O'Hara by a gate in the distance waiting for him. We see the entire family at dinner when all its members were together years before, and young Roddy reaching for a slice of bread when no one is looking and getting a gentle whack across the hand. We see the older brothers before they left for America, sauntering over a grassy glade of a Sunday afternoon, hands in pockets and peak caps on heads, singing. And we hear their unforgettable voices in a beautiful Welsh ballad. And finally we see little Hugh (Roddy) taking a Sunday walk with his father in the days before his father's death, the two of them coming to a summit, the father, cane in one hand, patting his boy's head with the other, then the two of them disappearing down the farther side. And then, sadly, The End.

This was my favorite of all films for many years, a great romance of lost loves and antiquities set against a lyrical landscape of Welsh villages, summer haze, and wonderful people. At the core of the film was the relationship of a small boy and his father, and since I had lost mine at an early age, perhaps this picture had a special meaning for me.

At any rate, after the births and the deaths, the family scenes together, the long, grueling strike, the harsh winters and the luxuriant springtimes, the departure of grown sons for a new world, the young hero, nearly crippled, learning to walk again, a first day in a new school, our young hero being taught how to box in order to lick the bully, the reprise at the end following the death of the boy's father represents one of the loveliest affirmations of life ever presented on the silver screen.

MEET JOHN DOE, 1941

⊙⊛⊛⊛⊛⊛⊛⊛⊛⊛⊛⊛⊛⊛⊛⊛⊛⊛⊛⊛⊛⊛⊛⊗⊙

In *Meet John Doe* Frank Capra achieved the next to final rung in his ladder to Utopia, a ladder to which less sentimentally idealistic viewers applied the epithet "Capracorn," and a Utopia that had more to do with the common man, individualism, democracy, human kindness, and small-town America than a faraway never-never land (*Lost Horizon* notwithstanding). The final rung was *It's a Wonderful Life* (1946), with James Stewart and Donna Reed. Capracorn it may well have been, but there was a pure, simple, albeit naïve, beauty to the man's thinking that has always appealed to me. He made movies that had a superbly crafted style and that were marvelously entertaining. Capra will always have a place in my pantheon of favorites.

The two great sequences that see the hero, that American of all Americans, Gary Cooper, first thwarted, then triumphant in bringing a real "government by and of the people" to the U.S.A. occur three quarters of the way through the picture and at the climax.

The first scene takes place at night at a crowded open-air stadium during a rainstorm. Thousands have come to hear Cooper speak because, over months of his radio addresses and personal appearances all across the country, they have come to identify him as the savior of America. His homespun simplicity, his candor, his understanding of the grievances and complaints of peoples everywhere have gained him almost messianic stature during his "campaign for truth." But corrupt, powerful Edward Arnold, the magnate who has given John Doe his platform because he feels the national support Doe is getting is the precise power he himself requires to achieve his own ends, moves in to stop Cooper from addressing the throngs who have come to hear him. He takes this action because Cooper will not bend to Arnold's wishes and publicly advocate a third national political party for the U.S.A. with himself (Arnold) as its leader. Clearly the magnate has profound aspirations toward the presidency.

And so as Cooper stands in the drenching rain, the dark night glowering all around him, thousands of umbrellas cloaking the field and benches, searchlights streaking the glistening gloom, forces move in to cut Cooper's microphone wires before he has a chance to respond to a scathing denunciation delivered in wet-faced, rimless-spectacled, fedora-garbed close-up by Arnold. Cooper vainly tries to tell the people that he (and they) have been pawns in the hands of a corrupt, power-hungry man. But they cannot hear him. Other Arnold aides provoke the crowds into near riot by hurling insults, apples, oranges, anything within reach, at John Doe. Wet, haggard, Gary Cooper stands in the rain in utter defeat and degradation.

The second scene takes place under the canopied top of the local city hall tower, and this is the climax of the picture. It is New Year's Eve and snow is quietly falling over the streets and buildings. Cooper is about to commit suicide, when the three key forces in his life appear from the shadows: Edward Arnold and men who want to prevent him from becoming a martyr to the people and hence destroying their fascist cause in America; James Gleason and his band of "little people" to whom he is a saint; Barbara Stanwyck, who discovers how he has been used by Arnold's special interests, loves him, and has come from a sickbed to stop him from killing himself.

The shot of Cooper carrying a collapsed Barbara Stanwyck across the floor of the tower, the snow falling behind him and the strains of Beethoven-Schiller's "Ode to Joy" growing louder on the sound track, this scene well earns its place on that list of great romantic moments that I carry among my film memories.

After Gleason warns Arnold from the entrance to the departing elevator, "You can't beat the people, Norton," the doors close and Capra cuts to New Year's bells ringing as his music reaches its climax. Then, as we go to final credits, the music switches to popular festive songs of the period like "Roll Out the Barrel" until the close.

LYDIA, 1941

❀❀❀❀❀❀❀❀❀❀❀❀❀❀❀❀❀❀❀❀❀❀

Merle Oberon wonders, "Who is the *real* Lydia?" on a balcony at the end of Alexander Korda's production of *Lydia* when, as an old woman, she has had the opportunity of meeting all her old boy friends again and of reminiscing over all of the different lives she led with them years before when she was young.

With one she had been purely platonic (like a sister), with another she had been a wild hellion, with another a confidante and a mother, and so forth, a veritable mosaic of personalities. And so she asks her old, faithful friend, Joseph Cotten, which of the different women was the *real* Lydia. And Cotten replies with the gentle sentimental wisdom of a valentine that there was no *real* Lydia, that she was *all* of them. It is a grand moment for lovers of stylish chestnuts and concludes a beautiful, richly textured love story.

Moments before, in an inner room, Lydia has been chatting to her admirers with natural concern and interest and hearty humor, but all the time awaiting the arrival of the one man she had never for so much as a day forgotten about through the long years. It is Alan Marshal, the Captain, the man with whom she had had such a tempestuous, passionate affair, the man who had stood her up at the altar and who had only returned now, after sixty years—at least he was *supposed* to join the reunion, Cotten had informed her. She cannot wait to see the love of her life once again. She has never married, has only thought of the Captain and awaited his return.

And then he arrives, and although old, he looks tremendously

94

elegant and romantic. As their hands unite and she looks into his eyes with the love of a lifetime, Marshal comments that she certainly looks familiar to him but that he can't quite remember her name.

CITIZEN KANE, 1941

◎◉◎◉◎◉◎◉◎◉◎◉◎◉◎◉◎◉◎◉◎

Citizen Kane, made by Orson Welles, is a cinematic cornucopia. The dazzling delights one finds within it are endless, each successive viewing revealing visual nuggets and philosophical insights missed the previous times round. It is one of the half-dozen or so films I always see whenever revived at festivals or on TV because it is so highly entertaining in its fusion of content and technical wizardry.

Citizen Kane is great fun, apart from being one of the most unusual and imaginative pictures ever made. It is a jigsaw-puzzle chronicle of a wealthy tycoon's life, eerie, mythical, remote, esoteric. And if it remains ultimately enigmatic, notwithstanding the next-to-last shot revelation of the secret of Rosebud (Kane's dying word and the flashback motif for the entire film), this is because *Kane* seeks to answer some of the basic questions of life itself.

The great visual moments in *Citizen Kane* are legion, but one of my favorites occurs near the opening when Kane dies. We have been given a slow series of moody, stark perspectives of Xanadu, Kane's castle-retreat in Florida complete with iron fencing and gates, towers, minarets, gables. Penetrating the only lighted window, we see Kane's lips in mammoth close-up uttering . . . "Rosebud" . . . then closing forever. We observe one of those now extinct glass balls that produce a falling snow effect when shaken slip from his fingers, roll down several carpeted steps (his bed is on a dais), then shatter on the marble floor. We note the figure of a nurse reflected on a glass shard from the broken ball as she enters the room and hurries to the dead man's bedside. We see her in silhouette pulling a sheet over his head. We get a long shot of the castle, the light from Kane's room still on, all else dark and unreal. Then the light goes out and the whole screen is plunged into blackness. Suddenly, before we get the chance to take another breath, in the blaring, trumpeting, heraldic style of one of those old "March of Time" news features, *News on the March* proclaims itself across the screen, and we find ourselves launched into a short news documentary—including suitably grainy, turn-of-the-century footage—on the life of Charles Foster Kane. This surely must be one of the great "cuts" in cinematic history. From death to life in a single blow, it jars and shakes the senses and becomes indelibly imprinted upon one's mind. But this is only the beginning.

Another fine moment in the film is the scene of the grand opening of the opera house Kane has built purely as a vehicle for his new wife, Susan Alexander. She is a very bad opera singer and her impresario, Fortunio Bonanova, knows this. Almost everyone knows this except Charles Foster Kane, who refuses to perceive her inadequacies because he is determined, as an extension of his own ego, that she will be a sensation. And so the curtain goes up on Mrs. Kane's debut. Welles shoots this sequence directly into the footlights, Susan in semi-silhouette against the blinding glare, Bonanova conducting from the canopied prompter's box in the floor of the stage.

As Susan sings, the camera tracks away from her in a vertical movement up into the flies. Higher and higher goes the camera, past yards and yards of ropes and teasers, the voice and the orchestra becoming slightly hollow and distant. Still the camera glides upward. Then, at last, it tracks up past the floor level of a scaffolding, where the feet and legs of two stagehands are observed. Still higher, and we see the two men in full form. Quietly, unobtrusively, one turns to the other and, in that most ancient of gestures, puts his thumb and forefinger to his nose to signify "she stinks."

Also in this film there is the incredible track shot over a building which is accomplished by the skillful fusion of a model and a real set by way of an "invisible seam" which cleverly conceals when you are leaving the one for the other. It is night and it is raining. The camera is outside the wet brick wall of a night club where Susan Alexander is appearing. Slowly the camera tracks up the exterior wall for two or three stories until it comes abreast of the roof. There, across from us, is a large neon sign proclaiming "El Rancho." The camera continues its movement, travels across the rooftop, and passes between letters in the sign. Then it swoops downward to the rain-beaded surface of a skylight. Lightning flashes (that's where the "seam" is located) and the camera moves through the glass picking up Susan Alexander and the film's anonymous reporter, William Alland, sitting at a dining table immediately below. The camera descends until it comes to rest on the two in medium close shot where a conversation is in progress.

Elsewhere in *Citizen Kane* there is the superb "breakfast" sequence, which consists of a series of dissolves, possibly seven or eight, each shot consisting of a phase of Kane's marriage, together covering about twenty years, carrying Kane from youth into middle age. In each of the episodes Welles and Ruth Warrick are filmed in profile and in medium close head-on shots at their breakfast table. As their gentle aging bears testimony to the passage of time from dissolve to dissolve, the pair become less amorous and gentle, more irritable, more distant, until in the last shot Kane no longer speaks to his wife, but simply, and brusquely, reads his morning paper. We know their marriage has all but evanesced.

A great sequence is located at the end when the secret of Rosebud is finally revealed, not to the characters of the screen, but to the movie audience. If you will remember, "Rosebud" was the last word uttered by Charles Foster Kane before he died. The whole film devotes itself to the efforts of a reporter to find out the meaning of the word within the context of Kane's life. The reporter never does, but in the last main sequence we (the camera) track across vast basement floors in Xanadu over piles and piles of art objects Kane had collected from all over the world. Finally we come upon two workmen putting junk into a great furnace to burn. A sleigh is seen on top of a pile nearest the furnace. "Put that in too," says one of the men. The other workman picks up the sleigh and throws it into the flames. This is the sleigh we saw young Charles Foster Kane playing with when he was with his father and mother in their home in the Midwest early in the picture. This is the sleigh with which he hit the wealthy lawyer, Thatcher, when the latter came to his home to take him to New York to be raised in affluent surroundings. This is possibly the only thing Kane ever really loved yet could not have. As the flames lick around the wood, the camera closes in and we see "Rosebud" printed in paint across its wooden surface. The flames continue to burn, the wood starts to turn brown, the paint begins to blister. Then, to the accompaniment of Bernard Herrmann's score, brilliantly dark and brooding and ominous, we see a long shot of Xanadu with the smoke from the chimney rising into bleak, early dawn skies. The shot dissolves to a pan down over a section of steel fencing where a sign—"No Trespassers"—makes its meaning clear. Then the final, angular shot over the "K" in the main gate of Xanadu and up to the black castle on the hill.

THE MALTESE FALCON, 1941

Although Carroll John Daly preceded him by several years, Dashiell Hammett is the name generally recognized today as the king of the "hard-boiled school" of American detective fiction. Raymond Chandler is, of course, right up there too, but it was Hammett who forged the blueprint for a whole era of writing whose tradition may still be traced in the modern-day works of Ross Macdonald and a few others. The effects of this "school" on other forms of American writing have been incalculable: wherever you find tough, taut, bald, hard, lean prose in a milieu in which pragmatic, existential survival dominates, you will find some scent of the legacy of writers like Daly and Hammett and Chandler. And probably nowhere can this "school," to go back to source materials, be rediscovered in more essential form than in, as Alexander Woollcott once termed it, that "granddaddy" of all tough American fiction, *The Maltese Falcon.*

Filmed first in 1931 with Ricardo Cortez as private eye Sam Spade, then in 1936 as *Satan Met a Lady* with Warren William and Bette Davis, the definitive version had to wait until the forties and the directorial genius of John Huston.

Who can ever forget the cast: Humphrey Bogart as Spade, Jerome Cowan as Miles Archer, Sidney Greenstreet as Gutman, Peter Lorre as Joel Cairo, Mary Astor as Brigid O'Shaughnessy, Elisha Cook, Jr., as Wilmer, and veterans Ward Bond and Barton MacLane as two detectives. Nor should we neglect a thirty-second performance by Walter Huston as a dying sea captain.

The scene that will always stand out in my mind takes place in Gutman's apartment near the end of the picture. This obese and greed-obsessed criminal has devoted two decades of his life to the search for a lost and priceless art object, a jewel-encrusted bird whose origins go back to the Crusades and the early days of the Knights of Malta. Spade gets the bird, wrapped in matted and shredded newspapers, from the dying captain of a burning liner moored in San Francisco's harbor, and hands it over to the fat man. Just watching Sidney Greenstreet tear away the newspapers, gaze upon and caress the bird, then start to scrape with a penknife at the darkish, leaden-looking coating on the bird in order to reveal its real bejeweled surface, perspiration beading his massive forehead, his face growing more and more anxious, his penknife scraping and chipping more wildly and feverishly as it begins to dawn upon him that there is nothing beneath the dark crust except more crust, that there is no jeweled surface, that in fact the object before him is a fake—just this one scene is worth the entire film.

ALL THAT MONEY CAN BUY, 1941

Walter Huston plays the Devil in William Dieterle's *All That Money Can Buy* as crafty, sly, whimsical Mr. Scratch, who sports a collapsed, crooked hat, smokes long, twisted stogies, and carries a little booklet in which he keeps track of the names of likely prospects for perdition. Also titled *The Devil and Daniel Webster,* the picture details Huston's pending claim over actor James Craig's soul during the course of a twenty-year "bargain" in which Craig is permitted to prosper materially and become a wealthy landowner. But the day finally arrives when old Beelzebub comes to "collect." However, at the last possible moment, Edward Arnold saves Craig from the fiery inferno and ostracizes the Devil from their presence.

In a final shot we find Huston sitting on a rail fence going through his booklet, page by page, looking for his next "prospect." Finally he looks up from his booklet and off screen, nodding to himself as he reflects upon the names he has just read. Then his eyes begin to scan slowly across the screen as he ruminates, eventually moving around until they come to rest directly upon us, the audience. Looking straight into the camera in gorgeous close-up, he stretches out his arm toward us and, wiggling his forefinger, he grins and gently beckons us to him.

WESTERN UNION, 1941

◎◎◎◎◎◎◎◎◎◎◎◎◎◎◎◎◎◎◎◎◎◎◎◎

There is something about the lather on Barton MacLane's face, the rough wood texture of the boardwalk outside the bar-bershop, the bleached paint on the barber's pole, the hardened mud street with glimpses of water in its wagon ruts, and the way that MacLane and Randolph Scott hold their guns that make the shoot-out at the end of *Western Union*, directed by Fritz Lang, a memorable event.

Scott, a good/bad man in this one, has been trying to pull away from his earlier cattle-rustling activities and particularly from the hold that his older brother, real bad man MacLane, has on him. He has been hired by Western Union's chief project en-gineer, Dean Jagger, to help run the first telegraph line across America, and grows to respect not only the job assigned to him but his colleagues as well. Foremost among these is engineer Robert Young, a greenhorn from the East whose adjustment to things western makes for much of the humor in the film.

But brother MacLane and his gang, in the pay of rivals, try to sabotage the project. In a last desperate measure they lure Scott to a rendezvous, bind and gag him, and then ride off to burn out Western Union's camp headquarters with a fire that all but con-sumes the movie screens upon which it is projected.

Randolph Scott rides into town to settle the score with his brother but is surprised in the entrance to a barbershop where MacLane is being shaved. Wily MacLane fires through the sheet draped around him in his chair, then comes out onto the street and stands over the dead body of his brother, but he does not have too long to be the victor. Robert Young, the easterner, his hair tousled and his face streaked with soot and ash from the forest fire caused by MacLane in the preceding sequence, approaches along the boardwalk from the distance to settle the score. Their gunfight is short but vigorous, and has the marvelously swift and deadly look of an old enameled cover of a Western story pulp magazine.

As Young delivers the lethal shot, MacLane's knees buckle and red-streaked discharges from his six-shooters go off into the dirt as he crumples from the boardwalk to the street.

Genie Rex Ingram holds Sabu in the palm of his giant hand in a truly magical moment from *The Thief of Bagdad*, 1940.

Errol Flynn roars into a final attack before his memorable death salute in *The Dawn Patrol,* 1938.

The gorilla is just off-screen and is about to terrify Laurel and Hardy on a Swiss bridge in *Swiss Miss,* 1938.

Early in the film this sequence, with Douglas Fairbanks, Jr., Cary Grant, and Victor McLaglen, indicates the scope of action lying ahead in *Gunga Din*, 1939.

A great bit of stunt work in the rip-snorting chase over the salt flats in *Stagecoach*, 1939.

Charlie·Chaplin as Adenoid Hynkel performs a maniac ballet with a globe of the world in a classic scene from *The Great Dictator*, 1940.

(San Francisco Chronicle)

The beginning of one of many fights between Brian Donlevy (right) and Akim Tamiroff that run all the way through *The Great McGinty*, 1940.

Mickey Mouse in a nightmare of water-carrying broomsticks in the classic "Sorcerer's Apprentice" sequence from Walt Disney's *Fantasia*, 1940.

Walter Pidgeon is trapped in a cave and builds a bow and arrow with which to slay super-Nazi George Sanders in the climax of *Man Hunt*, 1941.

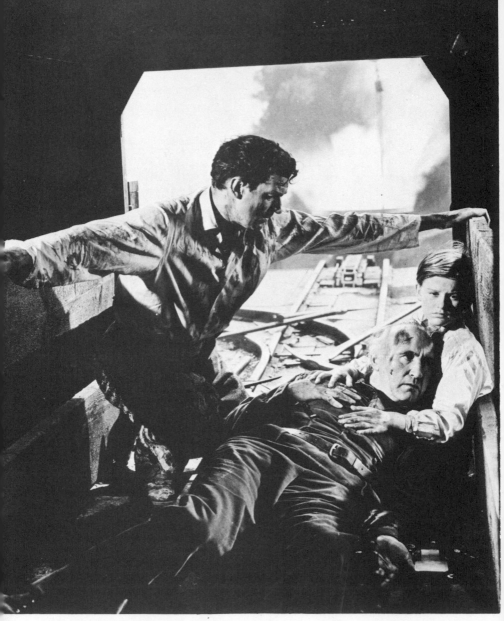

Roddy McDowall cradles the dead body of his father, Donald Crisp, while Walter Pidgeon kneels beside them in a coal mine elevator just before the unforgettable flashback montage in *How Green Was My Valley*, 1941.

Scotty Beckett and friend, playing Robert Cummings and Betty Field as children, say goodbye after school just before the change-of-time sequence on the fence stile in *Kings Row*, 1942.

Gary Cooper carries the collapsed body of Barbara Stanwyck across the snow-covered city hall tower on New Year's Eve at the end of *Meet John Doe*, 1941.

Ann Sheridan comforts Ronald Reagan as he discovers that his legs have been amputated in *Kings Row*, 1942.

Merle Oberon falls in love with Alan Marshal in one of the romantic flashbacks of *Lydia*, 1941.

Orson Welles (above) as Charles Foster Kane smiles sardonically in the now legendary breakfast montage from *Citizen Kane*, 1941. In another scene from the same movie (below), Kane delivers a campaign speech while running for governor of the state.

Humphrey Bogart (left), Peter Lorre, Mary Astor, and Sidney Greenstreet think they have found the long-sought bird in *The Maltese Falcon,* 1941.

Edgar Buchanan (far left), William Holden and Jean Arthur (the bride and groom), and Paul Harvey (long beard) in the wedding scene that leads to the gunfight that is never shown in *Arizona,* 1941.

Robert Cummings clutches the
sleeve of Norman Lloyd atop the
Statue of Liberty in the mind-
boggling conclusion to *Saboteur*,
1942.
(Museum of Modern Art/Film Stills Archive)

Joseph Cotten dances with Dolores
Costello while Tim Holt and Anne
Baxter rest on the stairs and the
camera begins its astonishing track
shot in *The Magnificent Ambersons*,
1942.

Edward G. Robinson is about to take a nap in his club before all the nightmares begin in *The Woman in the Window,* 1944.

ARIZONA, 1941

⊙⊙⊙⊙⊙⊙⊙⊙⊙⊙⊙⊙⊙⊙⊙⊙⊙⊙⊙⊙⊙⊙⊙

The preacher has just pronounced them man and wife; the town band has struck up a tune. William Holden, telling his new bride, Jean Arthur, to wait for him in the general store, has hitched on his gunbelt and, in his stiff black hat and his black wedding coat, is heading down the main street to shoot it out with Warren William, who waits, both six-shooters drawn, concealed around the corner of the saloon.

This is the climax in Wesley Ruggles' *Arizona*, one of the most spectacular, historically accurate, and underrated Westerns ever made. As Jean orders her groceries, we hear gunfire erupt in the distance. We are not permitted to see the source of action because that would have been inconsistent with the focus of the picture—a woman's perspective in the American West—and so the camera remains with Jean.

Fearful of the worst, holding back her tears, she continues to order, and in sporadic bursts the guns continue their roar. Then there is silence. Jean waits as though in a time suspension. There is another shot. Then total silence.

Jean Arthur, the camera very close upon her throughout this sequence, slowly allows her head to turn toward the door of the shop as we hear footfalls approaching down the wooden sidewalk. It is her husband, Holden, a handkerchief wrapped around one hand. She rushes into his arms.

KINGS ROW, 1942

⊚⊚⊚⊚⊚⊚⊚⊚⊚⊚⊚⊚⊚⊚⊚⊚⊚⊚⊚⊚⊚⊚

In Sam Wood's production of *Kings Row*, which was based on Henry Bellamann's novel, the "psychiatric lid" was removed from a small turn-of-the-century, midwestern American town for the first time in films. The picture, and the novel, emerged as a kind of anti-*Our Town* portrait, and yet there was a sweep, a dynastic pulse present that was as clearly romantic as anything Thornton Wilder ever wrote.

A favorite image of mine from the film relates to the device Wood employs to connote passage of time. He has his main characters—Robert Cummings, Ronald Reagan (I forget if Ann Sheridan and Betty Field were included in the following shots, but I tend to think not)—in early sequences in the story, when they are children, cross over a fence stile upon occasion, and he shoots this recurring motif by focusing his camera solely upon the legs and feet of the children as they mount the steps, cross over the top of the fence, and move down the steps on the far side. Cummings, incidentally, always does a little scuffing motion with his shoe toe at the top.

And then, after the camera has shown us the bare, teen-age legs and shoes of Robert Cummings mount the steps and move over the top—accompanied by Erich Wolfgang Korngold's marvelously evocative score—the scene dissolves to another pair of legs approaching the wooden steps and starting to ascend them, but this time long pants clothe the legs and the shoes are those of an adult. Korngold's score sweeps in with true fin-de-siècle stride, and the camera pans up to reveal Robert Cummings as a young man.

Counterpointing this effect is the later unforgettable scene in which Ronald Reagan wakes up after what he thought was minor surgery performed on an injured leg (some milk cans fell on him at the local railway depot), only to discover that family doctor Charles Coburn had gone ahead and amputated both of his legs. Reagan's histrionics were never more convincing than in this bloodcurdling sequence. Once seen, they can never be forgotten.

THE CAT PEOPLE, 1942

⊚⊚⊚⊚⊚⊚⊚⊚⊚⊚⊚⊚⊚⊚⊚⊚⊚⊚⊚⊚⊚

The Cat People was made by RKO under the production banner of Val Lewton, former script writer for David O. Selznick, and directed by Jacques Tourneur. Utilizing such economy measures as standing sets and contract players, this was the first of eleven pictures Lewton produced over the next four years, nine of which were tight, low-keyed little "B" budget horror affairs, dark of mood, usually given a modern setting, and possessing two, sometimes three scenes of real shock value. *The Cat People* contains two of my favorite horror moments.

In one scene Jane Randolph is shown swimming in a YWCA pool late at night. The pool is lit internally and is, hence, a bright rectangle in contrast to the black chamber in which it is located. Jane treads water in the center when, gradually, we begin to hear "something" moving ever so slowly around the black perimeter, something we cannot see but whose faintly rasping breath is audible to our ears. Our fear of the dark unknown mounts with that of the heroine until, in a vicious, invisible snarl, we hear Jane's bathrobe being clawed to shreds at the water's edge.

In another scene, Miss Randolph runs along an after-midnight roadway in New York's Central Park while, from the other side of a hedge flanking the street, we can hear—or we think we can hear—the soft sounds of padded feet gaining in momentum. The pace builds to a mild frenzy as Jane realizes she has nowhere to run, nowhere to hide. Then erupts the hissing cry that a cat makes leaping onto its prey, but it is only the air-controlled sound of a bus's doors opening beside her.

CASABLANCA, 1942

I doubt if Michael Curtiz ever remotely guessed, after he had shot *Casablanca,* that he had created a film whose fame would be as fresh thirty years later as it was then. Such are the ways of art and human taste. *Casablanca* was never more than a highly commercial, professionally well-tooled romantic drama, and yet its style and story chemistry were such and the appeal of its star (Humphrey Bogart) so great that it has become a Hollywood folk piece.

Its ending is still one of my choice scenes.

In a gently angled crane shot Humphrey Bogart and Claude Rains walk away from us across an airport tarmac shrouded in darkness, mist, and light rain, a scene ably mooded by Max Steiner's background score. Bogart has just dispatched the one woman he has ever really loved (Ingrid Bergman) by plane to America, and has just killed the sinister Nazi leader (Conrad Veidt) who had tried to apprehend her and her resistance-leader husband (Paul Henreid). Claude Rains, head of police, is an enigmatic man of whose political sympathies we are never sure until he orders his men at the airport to "round up the usual suspects" and, hence, lets Bogart go free. Realizing life in Casablanca will henceforth be too hot for both of them—it is World War II, after all, and France is under Nazi control—they head off together into an uncertain future. As we watch them move away into the fog, Bogart says to Rains: "You know, Louie, I think this is the beginning of a remarkable friendship." Steiner's music swells up, and the film ends.

SABOTEUR, 1942

⊙⊚⊙⊚⊙⊚⊙⊚⊙⊚⊙⊚⊙⊚⊙⊚⊙⊚⊙⊚⊙⊚⊙

A dark thread slowly and inexorably begins to unravel as a seam
in a coat sleeve splits and widens and the sleeve begins to tear
apart at the shoulder. The man in the coat is clinging for his life
to the area between the immense concrete forefinger and thumb
of the Statue of Liberty, but his main support comes from hero
Robert Cummings, who half crouches taut and tense immediately above him, one hand wrapped around a rung in the iron
railing which encircles the tiny platform at the base of the torch,
the other hand clutching his sleeve.

The man in the coat is Norman Lloyd, the saboteur of the
movie's title, and we are in Hitchcockland, high above New York
Harbor, playing out the last fiendishly suspenseful gasp of a wild
cross-country chase that began in a burning aircraft plant in Los
Angeles scant days before. Having been pursued by Cummings
to the top of the Statue of Liberty, Lloyd loses his balance and
slips over the guard railing to fall on the finger of the statue immediately below. Lloyd's body bounces slightly and slides down
toward the base of the thumb, then holds. Cummings climbs
down to rescue the spy, but is only able to grab onto the man's
coat sleeve near the wrist. Then the tiny rent appears in the
seam where the sleeve joins the shoulder and, agonizingly, the
suit begins to come apart. We see the two stark figures of the
hero and villain, windblown against a cloudy sky, from different
angles. Then we cut in to a startling close-up of Norman Lloyd's
wrist and hand slowly beginning to slide out of the sleeve
clutched by Robert Cummings. Back to the perspective shots of
the two figures high on the statue. Then to the ever widening
seam split. Then to Lloyd's perspiring, terror-stricken face. Then

to Cummings' visage of gaunt determination. Then to police boats arriving and uniformed officers running like flies across the huge pavement far below. Then in one last, horrifying shot we see the hand of the spy slipping suddenly out of the sleeve. Cummings freezes as the man, seen from a vertically downward angle (from our hero's point of view), falls away from us, his face contorted in screams, his body rotating awkwardly.

The picture ends as Cummings cautiously edges his way back up to the railing and to the waiting arms of Priscilla Lane.

Saboteur has at least one other gorgeous moment. It is the scene which opens with a close-up of two tough, deadpan faces of two enemy agents, seated in the front seat of a car crossing Boulder Dam. Robert Cummings is being "taken for a ride" in the back seat between master spy Otto Kruger and henchman Alan Curtis. But what makes the scene a gem is the opening shot of the two "toughies." With absolutely bland, hard faces, and betraying no emotion whatsoever, the two are singing in not-quite-flat monotones "Tonight We Love," the popular piece of the early forties based on the well-known theme by Tchaikovsky. The camera holds their faces, surmounted by snap-brim fedoras, for several moments, then moves between them to focus on the plight of Robert Cummings in the rear seat, the dull strains of the two thugs continuing in the background.

JUNGLE BOOK, 1942

⊚⊚⊚⊚⊚⊚⊚⊚⊚⊚⊚⊚⊚⊚⊚⊚⊚⊚⊚⊚⊚

Alexander Korda's films have always appealed to me for their fun and adventure. Basically, I suppose, it was the adroit combination of a literate script, the variety and frequently exotic nature of the locales, the strong sense of imagination in the plot lines, the excitement, the excellent casts, and the superb production values that accounted for this. *Jungle Book,* based on Kipling's Mowgli stories, is one of the best, and the last line of the film truly sums up everything that stands for adventure, romance, legend, and imagination in the cinema. Leading up to this line the two-hour film covers, in its Indian setting, the numerous adventures of a young boy, well played by Sabu, who is reared by the wild animals of his country's remote and dense jungles.

The whole odyssey is told by an ancient Hindu to an English lady who chances by his village hut and from whom the old one will gain a few pennies for his tale. Sabu's friends include elephants, crocodiles, and snakes and a young native girl whom he quietly grows to love. His enemies include the tiger and a sly, villainous native elephant herder portrayed to perfection by Joseph Calleia. Sabu rides elephants and glides down rivers clinging to the backs of crocodiles. He speaks to snakes and other creatures and they speak with him. He is at one with the great Indian forests and all creatures that live within them. In one long sequence he is forced to escort three greed-ridden men to a lost city of gold.

At the film's climax fire strikes the trees, set by the wicked Calleia, and Sabu must rescue all of the wild animals and escort them to an island in the middle of a great river, which is the only sanctuary from the inferno. The last shot we get of him is riding on the back of an elephant with the young girl he loves, leading a string of animals through dense blue smoke out into the river toward the sanctuary.

The film comes back to the present, to the old Hindu's hut where the tale is being told, and we realize for the first time that this old man is none other than the villain, Joseph Calleia. So he survived after all. But the English lady, excited by the tale she has heard, has a dozen questions to ask: "What happened to Mowgli? Did he get all the animals to safety? Did he eventually marry the young girl or not? What happened to the villainous elephant herder? Did Mowgli and he ever meet again? Did Mowgli grow up?" And so forth.

The camera closes in on Joseph Calleia's wrinkled, sly, grinning face, as he says: "That, mem-sahib, is another story."

And so the film ends.

THE PIED PIPER, 1942

⊙⊚⊚⊚⊚⊚⊚⊚⊚⊚⊚⊚⊚⊚⊚⊚⊚⊚⊚⊚⊚⊙

In *The Pied Piper* Monty Woolley plays a mild-mannered, retired English schoolmaster who crosses the English Channel on a holiday just before the outbreak of World War II and winds up leading a number of refugee children to safety. He undergoes a series of perils that would have defeated anyone less staunch of heart, but he performs these acts of bravery in total self-effacement.

After many adventures, the last scene in the film shows him back at his London club, comfortably ensconced in a large armchair, reading *The Times*. An elderly man nearby comments that Woolley has been away for a time. Woolley, following a long silence, still concentrating on his newspaper, nods lightly and says, "Yes." After a pause the man asks Woolley what he has been doing, and the latter replies, "Fishing." The colleague wonders "Where?", and again, after an interminable pause, Woolley responds, "Across the Channel." The man looks a trifle alarmed and asks, "Have much trouble getting back?" Woolley, his eyes still on his paper, answers, "Not much." The picture slowly fades.

THE MAGNIFICENT AMBERSONS, 1942

Tim Holt, as Georgie Minafer, eats pie throughout a long, single-take scene in Orson Welles's *The Magnificent Ambersons* while his Aunt Fanny, Agnes Moorehead, sits to one side of him and, in a high midwestern whine, talks with him about his family. Ray Collins as Uncle Jack hovers with chuckles and broad comments in the background.

The scene is set in the high-ceilinged kitchen of the Amberson mansion, and the mood carries a sensitive, haunting evocation of the turn of the century and a way of life swiftly departing forever. In creating this long, magical scene Welles apparently used improvisation, rehearsing his cast for days before the sequence was ready to be taken.

Chronicling the destructive effects of the automobile upon an aristocratic nineteenth-century American family, Welles's movie version of Booth Tarkington's novel has many stunning moments: Joseph Cotten's dinner table monologue about the impact of the new technology on all their lives; the last great ball (Anne Baxter and Dolores Costello were never lovelier) in which the camera moves with the elegance of the dancers past the potted palms and pillars and through room after room in the Amberson homestead in an astonishing track shot; the sleigh ride in the country, everyone so charmingly costumed in the best the period afforded, the lovers rolling in the snow, the laughter and excitement in getting Cotten's "horseless carriage" pushed and started, the touching camera "iris" (first used by D. W. Griffith in silent days: the scene closes to black in a steadily contracting circle) on the happy party as it chugs homeward through the snow; Ray Collins' farewell scene with Tim Holt in the railway station concourse, light streaming in long, slanted smoke rays down through multi-paned windows as the derby-hatted Uncle Jack expresses final feelings about his young nephew, then rushes off waving, club bag in hand, to catch his train.

YANKEE DOODLE DANDY, 1942
THE ROARING TWENTIES, 1939

Whenever Jimmy Cagney walks, runs, or dances across the silver screen a great moment happens. He has one of the world's stylish walks, combining ballet artist and Broadway hoofer, a dash of arrogance and "look at me, Ma" braggadocio. In any street scene he is magnificent simply to watch. But there were two very special moments that this walk was applied to, and they rank among the very best in cinema.

One occurred in *Yankee Doodle Dandy*, in which Cagney played George M. Cohan (Walter Huston played his dad). Like a marionette gone awry, Cagney flumps his way several times back and forth across an enormous stage in a scene from a big Broadway musical set in the Civil War. Two dozen or more beauties are behind him dancing. The music is "Yankee Doodle" and the sweep of the moment, with Cagney even walking up walls to do his turns, is quite breathtaking.

Another occurred in Raoul Walsh's *The Roaring Twenties,* in the climactic scene in which a wounded Cagney (he has just pumped Humphrey Bogart full of holes but has received the same in kind from Bogart's gang) is staggering along a New York street in winter. Snow is everywhere and the dying gangster runs and stumbles, almost seeming to lose his balance at times, trying to evade his pursuers, who have now been joined by the police. In his inimitable style, Cagney starts up an enormous set of steps leading to the entrance of a cathedral, finds when he attains a certain level that he can go no farther, begins to stagger-run back down the steps again at an odd angle, collapses on the snow, and dies.

JOURNEY INTO FEAR, 1942

The scene is a wet street at night somewhere in the Middle East. The camera is taking an angled upward shot of the half-lighted window of a cheap hotel. As the camera starts to move up toward the partly pulled blind and the strip of light coming through below it, we hear the high-pitched, somewhat squeaky voice of a tenor on an ancient record. The camera comes abreast of the window and we see a fat man (his name, if memory serves me, was Banat) in profile combing his greasy hair in front of a mirror. In the foreground the record is turning on an old-style Victrola. Then the record starts to repeat itself, pitching a high note over and over. The fat man finishes combing, shuts the record off, checks his German Lüger, dons a crushed hat whose brim goes down on all sides, and turns off the light. He goes to a door at the far end of the room and opens it, giving the screen a rectangle of light and making of himself a rather eerie silhouette in its brightness. He goes out and shuts the door. The screen is dead black. Then the title *Journey into Fear* blasts onto the screen with an appropriate background score.

So began the pre-credit footage of a film started by Orson Welles but completed and edited by Norman Foster, a highly underrated film craftsman, the same year. Welles was off to South America to do *It's All True*, which, sadly, was never finished. But *Journey* still carries much of Welles's imprint, including an ending on a rain-swept hotel ledge five flights above an Istanbul street. Welles also appears in the film as Colonel Haki, a colorful Turkish police chief.

THE OUTLAW, 1943

Looking back through the whole long history of the Western, I think that ironically the most underrated of all films in this genre must surely be Howard Hughes's production of *The Outlaw*. I say ironically because, while the picture was loudly and longly publicized in what is now vintage hype style, and is today still well known, *The Outlaw* is famous for all of the wrong reasons and seldom remembered for any of the right ones.

The film had censorship problems, mostly due to its sexploitive advertising campaign. It was not released until almost three years after its completion. But beyond the reams of press releases, behind the notoriety that the picture gained, and apart from Jane Russell's admittedly magnificent physical attributes (which dominate a good part of the movie), there lies a very funny, satirical, extremely unusual and individualistic, irreverent, tradition-breaking, and gorgeously photographed motion picture.

Some of its low-keyed, seemingly improvised acting anticipated the whole "method" scene of Brando and Dean in the fifties; its tongue-in-cheek humor and general ambience foreshadowed *Butch Cassidy and the Sundance Kid;* its satirical attitude toward its genre completely flew in the face of all its predecessors; and it represented what might well be the most important change in morals in the history of the screen.

In one long and memorable scene Doc Holliday (Walter Huston) and Billy the Kid (Jack Buetel) do nothing but sit at a table in a cabin eating pie and arguing about how they are going to divide the one horse and the one woman (Jane Russell) they have between them. At the end of the scene, Huston gets the horse and Buetel winds up with the girl. Huston appears pleased with his end of the bargain, but the Kid seems morose and dejected. "I sure liked that old horse," he mutters wistfully as the scene fades.

In another sequence of sheer bravura, Doc and Billy decide to "shoot it out"—this is to be the big, climactic duel, mind you—to the timing of a cuckoo clock. "When the clock cuckoos eight times we'll draw and fire," commands Doc Holliday. He pauses and then continues, "You know, men are really just kids after all. They play and fool, and then the playing gets rough and somebody gets hurt." He stares at the Kid solemnly. "This is where somebody gets hurt." A faint, fatherly grin creases his lips. "No matter how it turns out, let there be no hard feelings."

The clock commences to cuckoo. Gregg Toland's camera gives us a quick, staccato series of close-ups of fingers itching to draw, of eyes glaring intently, of gun butts protruding from holsters, all to the tune and face of the cuckoo clock. Finally comes the eighth cuckoo. Out pops the wooden bird doing its thing. Huston draws both his pistols in a lightning movement. But the Kid just stands there, his hands by his sides, sadness on his face. Huston warns, "If you don't draw I'll nick your ears!" Buetel doesn't draw. Doc aims one pistol with flourish, takes his time, fires. A startling close-up shows a chunk of the Kid's left ear lobe flitting away. "Do you want me to nick your other ear?" barks Holliday. No response from Billy, who simply stares at him. "Aw, gee, Kid," grins Holliday, putting away his guns and coming over to Billy and putting his arms around him.

Later, in a wild chase scene in which the Kid and his friends are pursued by savage Mescaleros, Victor Young's musical score utilizes a speeded-up version of Tchaikovsky's Fifth Symphony commingled with "Bury Me Not on the Lone Prairie." The screen is full of dust clouds as Billy and team drag brushwood at the ends of long ropes to confuse the Indians, and the background score has just the right sweep, rhythm, and mood of parody to complement its visual counterpart.

Still later, when Doc has been killed by Pat Garrett (Thomas Mitchell) and buried, Pat looks over at Billy, who has just put the last shovelful of earth on the grave mound and is tamping it down with his spade, and says, "Would you like to say a few words, Billy?" He pauses. "It's only fittin'." The Kid nods. They both doff their sombreros, bow their heads, and stare at the hump of black earth at their feet which houses their departed friend. There is an appropriate silence, then the Kid says, "So long, Doc." On goes his hat and the scene is over.

THE OX-BOW INCIDENT, 1943

⊚⊚⊚⊚⊚⊚⊚⊚⊚⊚⊚⊚⊚⊚⊚⊚⊚⊚⊚⊚⊚⊚

The Ox-Bow Incident, directed by William Wellman from the novel by Walter van Tilburg Clark, opens and closes lyrically with the same two men riding into a small western town and out of town, while in the background the strains of "Red River Valley" can be heard played by a harmonica. Held by this pastoral framing device, however, are scenes containing some of the grimmest and most ironic social realism ever filmed.

Unforgettable is the scene in the mountains where the posse of vigilantes, fresh from tracking down, capturing, trying, and hanging three cattle-thieving murderers, and now on its way back to town, runs into the sheriff. He informs the posse that the crimes had all been baseless rumor, that there had been no killing and no rustling, and that, consequently, the three men who had just been hanged were totally innocent. No viewer can ever forget the emotional impact of that moment.

Nor can one forget the following scene in the saloon where the posse stands, heads bowed along the bar, while Henry Fonda reads from a letter written by Dana Andrews (one of the three hanged men) to his wife. The simplicity, the touching humanity of this letter are almost too much to bear.

Moments later Fonda is out by his horse tightening the stirrups, getting ready to mount. His partner, Harry Morgan, rushes out to him, faces him over his saddle, and asks where he is going. "He said he had a wife, didn't he? He said she needed help, didn't he?" He mounts and, followed by Morgan, heads out of town.

SHADOW OF A DOUBT, 1943

ⓞⓞⓞⓞⓞⓞⓞⓞⓞⓞⓞⓞⓞⓞⓞⓞⓞⓞⓞⓞⓞⓞⓞ

Teresa Wright knows that her uncle, Joseph Cotten, has torn something from the evening paper that may well contain the answer to the growing mystery about his past and about his currently strange and menacing behavior. So she heads for the town library before it closes to study the paper for herself. The clock on the courthouse tower is almost at nine when she starts across the last intersection between her and her destination. But here, in classical Hitchcock tradition, a friendly traffic cop holds her back while he permits a line of cars to pass through, all while her eyes are on the great white face of the clock.

I WALKED WITH A ZOMBIE, 1943

Frances Dee leads a beautiful zombie (Christine Gordon) through acres of sugar cane toward the sacred ritual ground of a witch cult. Drums and voices echo in the night all around them, but we see nothing, only the figures of the two women moving in a track shot through the eerie gloom. We expect ungodly things to happen in the eternity of canes that fills the screen. The film is *I Walked with a Zombie;* the director is Jacques Tourneur; and the producer is the legendary man of horror, Val Lewton.

As Dee and Gordon move through the eerie fields of sugar cane, drums mounting ominously, the pair suddenly stumbles upon a skull gleaming with stark vacancy out of the darkness. And then a bit farther, and even more suddenly, the sinewy feet and legs of a black man appear before them. The camera pans up the body and finally comes to rest on the weirdly lit, somnambulistic countenance of Darby Jones, a zombie who has come to guide them to the unholy ritual.

FOR WHOM THE BELL TOLLS, 1943

Gary Cooper as Robert Jordan is mortally wounded at the end of Sam Wood's production of *For Whom the Bell Tolls,* based upon the Ernest Hemingway saga of the Spanish Civil War. Cooper stays behind to "hold" the pass while his beloved Maria (Ingrid Bergman) is carried away screaming by his comrades, Akim Tamiroff and Katina Paxinou.

Under the heat of an autumn sun Cooper lies behind his machine gun and waits for the government troops to show their heads over the edge of a ravine where a bridge has just been blown. He is in extreme agony but he controls his pain by thinking of Maria, and we can almost feel his doomed heart beating "against the pine needle floor of the forest," as Hemingway puts it in the novel.

When the troops appear, Cooper's perspiring face lines up behind the sight of the gun barrel, and his finger squeezes the trigger. The machine gun fires into the screen, the bursts of sound transcending reality and going into a hollow, echo effect. A gigantic bell ominously tolls in color silhouette. The End.

THE WOMAN IN THE WINDOW, 1944

One of the great, original mystery thrillers is Fritz Lang's *The Woman in the Window,* starring Edward G. Robinson, Joan Bennett, and Dan Duryea, with a nice D.A. role by Raymond Massey. Despite the fact that the picture's denouement came under critical fire for having utilized one of the oldest tricks in the world—Lang later defended his ending in an excellent essay—what led up to that final moment ranks among the most excruciatingly suspenseful sequences ever filmed, and hence has never been under question.

Robinson plays a university professor of psychology whose wife and family go away for a week's holiday. In his favorite club over dinner, Robinson discusses the psychology of the criminal mind with his close friend District Attorney Raymond Massey and another colleague. Then he takes a nap in his favorite chair, instructing the waiter to awaken him at a certain time.

Later that night in front of a store window Robinson, quite by chance, meets an artist, Joan Bennett, and through a series of quite natural circumstances sees her to her apartment. Robinson is a happily married man whose intentions toward Miss Bennett seem to be quite honorable; however, it turns out that she is the kept woman of a wealthy businessman who appears on the scene and mistakenly believes Robinson is making love to his mistress. The man engages Robinson in a scuffle which turns into a nasty fight, and very soon it seems that the man is going to throttle Robinson. But the professor, in a totally self-defensive action, gets hold of a pair of scissors and jabs them wildly into the man's back. The man dies, right then and there, before the stunned couple; the professor realizes that the circumstantial evidence would be too damaging and that he could never extricate himself from the web of incriminations a prosecuting attorney would draw around him; therefore, he decides the only solution lies in hiding the deceased in some other locale.

To make a long tale of superbly built anxiety short, he follows through with his plan, only to become invited later ironically by Raymond Massey to join him in solving the case when the body is discovered in a suburban woodland.

As various clues become uncovered and guilt-ridden Robinson imagines ever more vividly the finger of the law swinging inexorably toward him, a sleazy, yancey character portrayed by Dan Duryca turns up—he had witnessed the whole tragedy from his window—and commences to blackmail the professor and Miss Bennett. Robinson drains all his private savings to keep the man quiet, but as the man's insatiable demands increase, Robinson and Miss Bennett, with no one to turn to, no one who would ever understand their moral innocence, are driven scene by scene toward ultimate despair.

Finally, as we approach the sequence that I shall long remember, Robinson is forced to tell Duryea there is no more money left to give him. Duryea tells Robinson and Bennett he is going to turn them in and departs from their rendezvous to do so. Robinson now knows there is no hope, no way out. He bids farewell to Miss Bennett—his face indicating quite clearly what he intends to do—and returns to his flat. Bennett then heads home along the wet, dark streets with which the film abounds. In his apartment Robinson takes a parting look at photos of his wife and child, then goes to the bathroom for a glass and a certain bottle. He takes these back to his living room, places them on a table, sits down, and contemplates them. Then he pours the liquid from the bottle into his glass.

Meanwhile, en route to her home, Joan Bennett hears wailing sirens and, rounding a corner, encounters a whole cluster of excited people in the center of the road. When she pushes through the crowd and looks down at the cause of the excitement, she beholds in sheer astonishment the crumpled and quite dead form of Dan Duryea. The blackmailer has been killed.

Instantly she runs to a pay phone to alert the professor about their incredible good fortune. The threat hanging over their heads has been removed. There is now no one to connect them to the man who died in her rooms. They are finally, completely free. Mentally praying she is not too late, she puts change into the coin slot and dials Robinson's number. The line rings and rings and rings. Her face grows white and tense. This is surely one of the great moments in all film suspensedom. Is she too late?

The camera cuts to the professor's flat, pans across furniture, and finally alights on the table by his chair. There, in close-up, stands the empty bottle, and there, beside it, the empty glass. Then, as the phone's ringing mounts to an emotional crescendo in the minds of the audience, the camera pans over to the chair and to Robinson. His face is motionless and slightly at an angle to us. Is he dead? Was Joan Bennett too late? The ringing persists and the camera closes in for an intense, intimate shot of the unfortunate, despairing professor, quite possibly the highest peak of tension in the history of movies.

A hand reaches down from off screen and shakes Robinson gently. The camera dollies back from his deadly still face and we discover we are no longer in his apartment but in the club where we were early in the film. A waiter is awakening him from his nap. The entire movie has been a dream!

As Robinson rouses himself, gets his hat and coat, and leaves the club, we notice that the man who hands him his coat is none other than the man he murdered in his dream and—delight of delights—the doorman, resplendent in greatcoat, brass buttons, and embroidered cap, turns out to be Dan Duryea.

Down the wet, dark street, at the very store window containing the painting of a woman where he had stopped earlier in his dream and where Joan Bennett had appeared from nowhere and asked for a light, a voice from off screen *again* asks for a light.

Robinson freezes in terror and stares in wide-eyed horror in the direction of the voice. For a moment we believe it is Joan Bennett and that the whole dreadful nightmare of murder and blackmail is about to take place all over again.

But it is only a prostitute, cigarette in hand.

Muttering something like, "A light?—Oh, no, no, no—" Robinson clutches his hat to his head and rushes off down the middle of the pavement in frenzied flight. Finis.

Despite the negative reaction from many reviewers at the time, I found this ending amusing and ironical. It was a real joy to discover that the professor, whom we had grown to like and be truly concerned about as the story unfolded, did not have to pay for a crime that he was morally innocent of performing. Lang's later defense of the film was along these lines.

On another level, and by virtue of the fact that quiet, mild-mannered Edward G. Robinson actually dreamed the dream we saw depicted on the screen, Fritz Lang is able to suggest something of the not-so-quiet frustrations and dark desires that can lie beneath the surface of even the most gentle of civilized souls.

SINCE YOU WENT AWAY, 1944

One of the most extraneous scenes ever filmed, and yet one that is possessed with much surprise, charm, and magical wit, occurs somewhere in the middle of David O. Selznick's wartime love story, *Since You Went Away*.

For no reason at all, the camera cuts from our star performers (Jennifer Jones, Monty Woolley, Claudette Colbert), who are seated in their fashionable middle-class home, to the lawn out back. The large, lovable, pug-ugly bulldog is seen lying on the grass, his paws over his nose, sleeping. It is a beautiful afternoon in summer. A short distance away stands a water sprinkler, inert and inactive. The scene is a pure, photographic still life. Suddenly the sprinkler goes on, water flies everywhere, and the dog jumps up and scoots off. That's all.

THE MIRACLE OF MORGAN'S CREEK, 1944

⊚⊚⊚⊚⊚⊚⊚⊚⊚⊚⊚⊚⊚⊚⊚⊚⊚⊚⊚⊚

From the behind-the-credits footage of Preston Sturges' *The Miracle of Morgan's Creek,* we are told that a miracle has occurred in a small American town, but we have to wait till the climax of the picture two hours later to find out what it was. It is here that a high point in visual comedy transpires.

Wife Betty Hutton goes to the hospital to have a baby and husband Eddie Bracken goes to visit her. It should be indicated that Bracken, throughout the course of the film, has been a failure at everything he has tried, and that at this point in the movie his fortunes, by one mad circumstance or another, have reached their nadir.

As he proceeds through the foyer of the hospital a nurse asks him if he would like to take a look at his offspring on his way to his wife's room. He nods yes, naturally, and moves along a hall with her until they come to a broad glass window which looks into the newly born babies' ward. Bracken is getting pretty excited and wonders, as he stares through the glass plating at half a dozen cribs, which baby is his. He pantomimes this question to the nurse behind the window and she in turn pantomimes the answer. With a spread of both her arms and a great, generous smile she indicates that *all* six babies are his. That's right! *All six!* Wife Betty Hutton has had sextuplets. Bracken goes berserk with shock, swings on hospital chandeliers, flies over furniture. Later, when news of the historic event is broadcast around the world and the screen erupts in a montage of reactions, one newspaper bears the headline: CANADA DEMANDS A RECOUNT! Lovely.

THE GREAT MOMENT, 1944

The Great Moment has a great moment at that particular position in its running length where many of the great moments contained in this chronicle are found: at the climax. Largely neglected by the public and by film critics alike, this film is really
one of Preston Sturges' best, although perhaps too offbeat in its
mixture of farce and sobriety for popular consumption.

It details the main events in the life of a dentist named Morton,
the discoverer of anesthesia, and while I have no way of knowing how biographically accurate the film is, I do know that this
need not necessarily be the main concern of the director. Sturges
was always up to comic satire, and everything—even a man's life
—was fodder to his purposes. Here he puts Joel McCrea in the
title role and in one of the most delightfully bizarre fusions of lunacy and seriousness—after all, anesthesia is not exactly everyone's idea of a colorful topic—employs great dolpings of farce
and burlesque to achieve his ends. These last two items are
standard Sturges tools, and whereas in other hands their use in a
biographical film of this kind might have been pure disaster,
here they are brilliantly used to heighten the outright medical
obstinacy and arrogance faced by McCrea.

One splendid moment occurs when our experimental doctor is
crawling around the floor of his home, a cloth that has been
liberally dipped in a kind of alcohol-cum-chloroform solution in
one hand, attempting to apprehend the family cat and experi-
ment upon it. What happens is that our hero becomes slowly,
inexorably pie-eyed in the process.

His administering of a kind of laughing gas to dental patient
William Demarest is wonderful to behold. After roaring his head

off Demarest goes berserk, runs down a long hall, and goes right out through a plate-glass window, falling down two stories through a canvas awning and landing in a policeman's arms.

His banterings with his loyal wife, Betty Field, are also a joy to experience throughout the film.

But my favorite sequence is, as already indicated, at the end. The entire medical profession is opposed to the kind of anesthetic McCrea has developed, and forbids its use. At film's climax, in a large American hospital, McCrea is standing beside the stretcher bearing the body of a young boy who is due within moments to undergo a serious and painful operation. Observing the look upon the boy's face, a look that quietly cries out for help, McCrea decides there and then that he will simply not permit this child to endure the kind of pain accepted as natural by the medical establishment of the day in its no-anesthetic stance. McCrea takes the boy's hand and, as the doors to the surgical amphitheater swing open and the stretcher is wheeled in before the solemn gazes of dozens of doctors and students who have gathered for observation purposes, he walks in by his side. The film ends as the doors close behind them.

DEAD OF NIGHT, 1945

⊙⊙⊙⊙⊙⊙⊙⊙⊙⊙⊙⊙⊙⊙⊙⊙⊙⊙⊙⊙⊙⊙

There are few motion picture anthologies equal to *Dead of Night* for sheer style and coherence, and very, very few films of the weird or horror or uncanny variety to approach it in its use of apprehension, the bizarre, and out-and-out fright.

Although *Night* employs the work of four different directors (Cavalcanti, etc.), a marvelous unity of purpose prevails; in fact it is one of the few omnibus pictures on record in which all the disparate elements tie together.

The great screen moment within the two and a half hours of this film is a split or cyclical moment, one half of which occurs at the beginning, the other half at the end. In the first shot we see a long line of trees bordering an English country lane. The view is one of perspective with the trees beginning close to the screen and receding into the distance. A car is moving along the lane toward us; it stops near us and a middle-aged man gets out and stares across a patch of moorland. In the distance he sees a house, really an estate with a large Tudor-style central mansion. He gets back into his car and drives up a narrow roadway toward it. A fairly ordinary opening, you might say. Well, hold on.

When he arrives at the house, we discover that he is an architect and has been summoned by the host for some sort of consultant work, but what really interests him (and us) is the oddly assorted gathering of people who have come to the mansion as guests for the weekend.

Each one of them, our hero feels, he has seen before in a dream, and he tells them so. This prompts a series of curious tales, five in all in the original uncut version, each imaginatively bizarre, one wildly funny, and one or two downright horrendous.

134

As the stories progress, the hero feels, during the interlocking sequences, that he is compelled to do something of which he has no knowledge and which he cannot control. In the end, after we have lived in a room with a mirror that looks into the past century, after we have ridden on a doomed bus, after we have committed suicide, returned from the dead, witnessed murder in a children's game and discovered a lost attic, and finally watched a dummy take over the personality of his ventriloquist-master after the master has tried to "murder" the dummy by crushing his body to sawdust, we observe our hero being compelled by some unknown force to murder one of the house guests, a man he barely knows and does not hate.

As this gruesome scene is in its act of completion, we hear an alarm clock ring and—behold—our hero wakes up in his London home. His wife is beside him, worried, because he has apparently tossed and turned so feverishly in his sleep. He has had the "same dream all over again," he explains, the same people, the same build-up to the same ghastly finish.

Tea is served. The husband and wife begin to relax and discuss their plans for a Saturday and Sunday by the sea, when the phone rings and "someone" invites the husband on a business project down to his house for the weekend. The husband explains he has a prior commitment, but says he will call back with a definite answer later. He turns to his wife as we, the audience, begin to grow uneasy. Which shall it be, he asks her, a holiday or work? They decide he should flip a coin. Heads he takes his wife to the sea, tails he accepts the business offer. He flips the coin, looks at it, then stares quizzically into the screen, music mounting hauntingly behind him.

And now for the last scene of the film: a long, familiar line of trees bordering an English lane, and a car approaching us. The car stops near us and the hero gets out and stares across a patch of moorland. And there, in the distance, in a shot that makes us shudder, is the same large Tudor-style house we saw at the beginning. "The End" cuts across our view.

THE LIFE AND DEATH
OF COLONEL BLIMP, 1945

Deborah Kerr plays three different women, all of them remind-
ing Roger Livesey of his first lost love, in Pressburger and Powell's *The Life and Death of Colonel Blimp*, an epic drama of a
man who does not adjust to the changing times. The film follows
his family and military life from Victoria's last years to World
War II, including his romantic life and his friendship for a German, Anton Walbrook, which spans several decades. But it is
England, and the best of England, that dominates in this film of
tradition and honor and gallantry and respect for one's friends
and one's country.

There are three splendid moments: (1) The long, carefully detailed preparations for a fencing duel between Livesey and Walbrook (this was how they first met; Walbrook was the surrogate
or deputy for the German military officer whom Livesey detested
and with whom the duel was arranged), which consume about
eight screen minutes in a large gymnasium in Berlin just after
the turn of the century and which lead into the actual duel itself.
Ahhh, but here's the twist! The duel only manages to get started
—a few parries and positions—when the camera gently pans
away from its two combatants and moves up through the rafters
of the gymnasium and high upper windows to show the snow
quietly settling over the city outside. We never see the duel. We
dissolve to a hospital a few hours later where both men are in
adjoining beds, bandaged up to their noses, and in excellent
humor. (2) The passage of time handled by having trophies of
the busts of wild animals "pop" out of Livesey's game-room wall,
the years and locations clearly connoted beneath. (3) The pause
at the stoplights in a military limousine at night during World

War II, with the two old friends, Livesey and Walbrook, united again after ten years, reclining in the rear seat, the red glare of the lights reflecting upon the face of the young WAAC who is driving the van, and Livesey noting in her half-turned face the look of the two women who had meant most to him during his long life. Deborah Kerr plays the driver, just as she had played the roles of the two women in earlier scenes. Livesey wonders if Walbrook can see the resemblance, but he finds it difficult in the half darkness to do so. Then we see a culvert and a pond in autumn, and brown leaves are skitting over the surface of the water and the voices of Livesey's lost loves are speaking to him. He is old now, very old, and the moment is properly, magnificently sentimental.

ISLE OF THE DEAD, 1945

⊚⊚⊚⊚⊚⊚⊚⊚⊚⊚⊚⊚⊚⊚⊚⊚⊚⊚⊚⊚⊚⊚

The retelling of this next great moment from the cinema not only reveals it to be my very favorite terror/horror sequence of all time, but also indicates, as I said in the introduction, the non-objective role that memory plays in reconstructing past events.

The picture is *Isle of the Dead* (I didn't see it until 1953) and the producer was Val Lewton. The scene is the one in which the woman is buried alive in a pine box in a Grecian crypt. Boris Karloff, cast this time as a benevolent Greek general, and the other diverse characters who find themselves quarantined on an island off the coast of Greece during a plague do not notice the woman's left eyelid twitching after she has collapsed and supposedly "succumbed." But we the audience know she is still alive; a close-up has enabled us to see the telltale eyelid. And we remember the worries she expressed in earlier portions of the film, worries about falling into a catatonic trance and being presumed dead, and then being buried alive. We also remember her urgent pleas, upon those occasions, for an application of the "feather" and "mirror" tests to her mouth (in order to determine whether or not breath and hence life exist within her) should she ever appear to die. We are well alerted, well warned. But not Karloff and the others. They have forgotten.

And so they put her into a large pine box and carry her to the crypt.

Later in the film, and in the dead of night—as I have recounted to friends over the years—the camera gets into one end of the long death chamber and focuses on the coffin at the other end. All is still and silent save for the tiny, muted explosions occasioned by drops of water from a crack in the stone ceiling fall-

138

ing onto the wooden lid of the box containing the "dead" woman. Then, slowly but relentlessly, the camera begins to track forward across the great floor of the crypt toward the coffin. A strain of eerie music, imperceptible at first, gradually insinuates itself upon us. Drop . . . drop . . . drop goes the water in quiet booms upon the lid. The music begins to increase in intensity and we continue our irresistible march toward the box, which looms larger and more ominous in our screen vision as we get closer and closer to it. Finally the camera comes to rest when the coffin occupies the entire frame of the screen. The music reaches a background crescendo. We stare stupefied, frozen in terror, waiting for something to happen. Suddenly—the music cuts. Then—*nothing* happens. Having been carried to an insane pitch of anxiety, we are permitted instant relaxation. We sigh . . . that is, for about one-and-a-half seconds we sigh. And then, just as an enormous letdown is about to overcome us, there bursts from within the coffin the damnedest screaming and shrieking we have ever heard, followed by a maddening scratching and clawing from inside the lid.

We are caught off guard. All of the emotion previously built up returns with such a sudden thrust that we are very nearly jolted out of our seats. Then nails begin to rasp and screech as the occupant of the coffin starts to force up the wooden lid. Later the woman emerges to wreak havoc on those around her until she finally commits suicide in the sea, but for us the great moment is over. And that is the moment that has lived with me for over two decades and which I have described to friends so many times.

Not too long ago the film was revived as a late, late, late show on local television. I had not seen the picture during the intervening years and was therefore anxious to view it again and relive my favorite scene. Accompanied by a colleague who had never seen the original but had heard me recount the plot many times, I stayed up until 3:30 A.M. to catch it.

What I saw was indeed *Isle of the Dead*, but when we came to the important scene, I was dumbfounded, for what I saw transpire before my eyes was *not at all* the scene I had been recounting for twenty years. Oh, they buried the old girl in a coffin, all right, and the crypt was of the same stony dimensions and mood that memory had dictated, but beyond this similarities ceased.

Right off the top, as soon as the coffin bearers had departed from the tomb, a shrieking and scratching had erupted from inside the box. No build-up, just shock. Then the main action continued in the house for a few moments. Then we were back in the crypt taking a close view of the coffin. Water was drip-drip-dripping from a crack in the roof and exploding off the lid of the box, but there was no music whatever in the background. Once more we cut to the interior of the house, with Karloff and colleagues deep in dialogue. Then back to the coffin again, and again a close view but from a slightly different angle this time and with a faint forward movement in the camera shot. But still no music. Back to the house; back to the coffin. Several repeats of this shooting rhythm, each with minor angle alterations and barely suggested movements toward the coffin. Then there is the squeaking of the lid—this jars us—as it is pressed upward from within. But no long, uninterrupted track forward, and no rising crescendo of music building up to a sudden and dead silence which causes the viewer to let his guard down long enough to have the hell scared out of him. What had I really seen twenty years before? And what had happened during the intervening years?

The reason the "great moment" from *Isle of the Dead* is included in this collection is precisely the same as for all the other "great moments." They are personal memories from the cinema as I saw it, culled from over forty-five years of movie-going, and what has been put down here respecting this particular film is my memory of the most frightening screen moment of my life. No matter if the empirical data observed with a witness at three-thirty one morning via TV should fly in the face of my remembrances of shots past.

Fair enough, then: so much for my determined, personal—albeit spurious and irrational—reason for being unwilling to complete this book without including this particular memory with its ambience of darkness, fear, and morbid fantasy. The scene had simply meant too much to me over the last quarter century, had been dwelt upon by me and recounted to so many friends and acquaintances, that it *had to* go into the collection. If it was all to be a myth in the final analysis, then it was a myth I solemnly refused to part with.

So much for the personal. There happens to be another reason why this "great moment" is included here.

Not long ago I was addressing a small group on how personal bias affects what one sees and retains, and I used *Isle of the Dead* as an example. At the end of the lecture a chap came up to me and introduced himself as a cinéaste, although he did not use that word, and stated that my original memory of *Isle of the Dead* had been correct, that he had read somewhere, years before, the picture had been briefly withdrawn from distribution at some later time because the scene in question had "really been too much" for some audiences and had been re-edited. Unfortunately he could not give me the name or location of his source-reference material, nor the year of re-editing. Remember—I had not seen the film until 1953.

Later, a colleague showed me an extract by James Agee, from a book on the horror genre, and there, by Harry, is a description of the great scene in basic outline almost identical to my memory version. The long track forward is there, but the chief difference would appear to be an absence of background music in Agee's version. And Agee's version, like my own, was *not* the treatment I saw that early morning on television.

And so the mystery still persists. The real truth probably lies somewhere down the middle of all that I have recorded here. Possibly the film *was* re-edited as that fellow at the lecture had indicated and I was therefore vindicated. But also, most probably, I had performed some mental alterations on the scene, as I have been maintaining all of us do on everything we see. After all, I say there was music and Agee says there was no music . . .

THE BODY SNATCHER, 1945

⊚⊚⊚⊚⊚⊚⊚⊚⊚⊚⊚⊚⊚⊚⊚⊚⊚⊚⊚⊚⊚

Under the combination of producer Val Lewton and director Robert Wise, *The Body Snatcher* emerged as one of the great classics of the horror genre, containing three of the most macabre moments ever filmed. The film was adapted from a short story by Robert Louis Stevenson, based on history's famous pair of murderous ghouls, Burke and Hare.

Karloff's painfully slow and chilling build-up to the suffocation (which the actor calls "Burking") of an eavesdropping servant, Bela Lugosi, is one. Before the final shot where he smothers Lugosi by placing one hand over the servant's face in such a manner as to block air from entering both his nose and his mouth, Boris injects the odd jig into the sequence and even chants an excerpt or two from Scottish ballads, all as a prelude to the final terror.

Elsewhere in the picture there is a fine long shot showing a street singer moving away from us through a great stone archway and disappearing into the shadowy fog beyond, her voice carrying a plaintive tune as she goes. Following her is a horse-drawn cab, and this vehicle, too, vanishes into the swirling mists beyond the archway, the ominous click of the horses' hooves faintly receding in the night. The camera remains focused on the cavernous archway, nothing visible except the fog, no sound save the street singer's distant strains. And then, without warning, her song is abruptly cut off.

At the end of the film, Henry Daniell, who uses fresh corpses for dissection purposes, kills his prize ghoul, Boris Karloff, and dissects him. But he becomes haunted by the dead man. Weeks later, when returning by buggy across a Scottish moorland from robbing a new grave, a drenching rain scouring the crags and bracken, he goes out of his senses. First he hears Karloff's voice mounting with the rhythmic momentum of the cab. Slowly the freshly retrieved corpse in the canvas sacking behind him works loose and flounces against him. Shrouded in the wet gloom of the buggy, whipping his horses with maddening fervor, Daniell begins to imagine that the body of Boris is in the bag. He finally inspects it with a lantern and then—in one memorably horrific shot—the stark, dead, waxen-moistened face of Karloff crashes onto the screen. Of course Daniell goes completely to pieces, and dashes himself and the buggy over a cliff.

THE SPIRAL STAIRCASE, 1946

In the parlor of a small New England hotel at the turn of the century, a screen flickers with the tattered images of a silent movie. The setting is a seaside; a woman is drowning and a brave young man is about to swim to her rescue. The action is accompanied by the clinking music of a piano played by a spectacled woman whose eyes constantly dart from keys to screen.

The camera shifts perspective now, slowly craning upward until it leaves the parlor and moves past the chandelier and ceiling and into a dimly lit bedroom above. A woman is preparing for bed. She undresses, goes to the closet for her nightgown—the piano faintly underscoring from below the silence and loneliness of the room—then returns to the center of her quarters to slip the garment over her head. But the camera remains focused on the open closet from which she has departed. We sense something is wrong with the closet but have no proof of what we feel. It is a normal closet with dresses on hangers all in a row. And still the camera remains. Only a few seconds have elapsed and yet we feel apprehensive.

Then, quietly but relentlessly, the camera begins to track forward toward the dresses. As we approach the rack we see that the camera has selected for its target a narrow space or parting in the clothes with only jet blackness behind. We grow tense, wondering what is lurking in that gloom. We move closer and closer until we move right into and through the black space and find ourselves staring into a human eye. The eye grows larger and larger the closer we get until it fills most of the screen and there, in a faint hue upon its pupil, we see the woman pulling the nightgown over her head. A quick cut to a close-up of the woman's hands protruding from the top of the garment in an effort to pull it down over her shoulders suddenly reveals the hands going rigid and clawing hideously at the air. We know what is happening. And that was the way Robert Siodmak began *The Spiral Staircase*.

THE CHASE, 1946

⊙⊙⊙⊙⊙⊙⊙⊙⊙⊙⊙⊙⊙⊙⊙⊙⊙⊙⊙⊙⊙

In Arthur Ripley's film *The Chase*, Steve Cochran loves to climb into his great sausage of a limousine and race express trains. He is a gangster, and a sado-masochist, and he lives in a mansion in the country not far from a multi-mile stretch of highway that runs abreast of a railway track. At the far end of the stretch, the road turns abruptly and crosses the track, and it is here that Cochran gets his greatest kicks, for at this point he is able to assert his final supremacy over his adversary by roaring over the crossing microseconds ahead of the engine.

If this were all there was to the recurring sequence, it would still represent some fairly memorable suspense. But there is one other element that Ripley injects that carries the concept far beyond the ordinary. It is this: attached to the floor of the rear seat of his limousine, Cochran has a flat metal box with a hinged lid which he can flip open with the flick of his foot. Inside this box are a gas pedal and a speedometer. Whenever chauffeur Peter Lorre shows signs of letting the train creep ahead, Cochran presses a button that closes the glass partition between himself and Lorre, thus sealing off the latter from any communication with him. Then he opens the box and begins applying his foot to the gas pedal.

The next moment, just when Lorre begins to realize what is happening, Cochran presses another button and all brake control from the front seat is cut off. As the car gains maddening speed, Lorre pumps the brake pedal, and nothing happens. His face twitches in lunatic fashion, and his forehead becomes dotted with perspiration. Lorre never gets used to this recurring trick of

Cochran's. He tries to plead with his chief, but the gangster is behind a closed partition and only smiles at him.

Without any form of brake control, and traveling too fast to even consider jumping, all Peter Lorre can do is steer, while Cochran presses the gas pedal harder, and harder, and harder.

They always manage to get over the signal crossing just in the nick of time, that is except the last time. . . .

HENRY V, 1946

⊚◎◎◎◎◎◎◎◎◎◎◎◎◎◎◎◎◎◎◎◎◎◎

The horses begin at a leisurely pace, their armored fifteenth-century riders sitting almost casually in their saddles, their shields glinting in the morning sun, their lances upright. We see them in profile, the camera moving with them, focusing its lens in depth down their long flank. After ten or fifteen seconds during which the pace of the cavalry slightly increases, we realize that the camera has no intention of altering this relationship but is going to maintain its perspective and move forward with the gathering momentum of the battle line. The result may well be the most spectacular shot of its kind ever put on film. From a slow pace to a maddened fury, we watch the speed of the cavalry grow second by second into a full-scale charge, horses and riders thundering toward the French line at Agincourt, heads bent in determination, lances forward. Laurence Olivier was the director of this big scene in his production of Shakespeare's *Henry V*.

BRIEF ENCOUNTER, 1946

⊚⊚⊚⊚⊚⊚⊚⊚⊚⊚⊚⊚⊚⊚⊚⊚⊚⊚⊚⊚⊚⊚⊚

Trains pass through lonely stations, disturbed only by the hiss of steam and the blast of the whistle, in David Lean's production of *Brief Encounter*. Through artful repetition of this visual theme the director and cameraman (Robert Krasker) establish and deepen a poignant mood that has the quality of long-lost valentines (minus the treacle). This mood is in perfect consonance with the story of middle-aged romance between Trevor Howard and Celia Johnson.

Perfect, too, is the ending, in which Celia cannot bring herself to confess her affair to her husband, though it was not consummated. She simply stares into space while Rachmaninoff's Second Piano Concerto plays in the background. She is oblivious to her husband's profound concentration upon her. This concentration subtly reveals to the viewers that he inwardly surmises what has been happening over the preceding weeks. He is, however, as reluctant as she is to make his feelings explicit and can, therefore, only say to her as he puts his arms around her in the film's last shot, "You've been away for a long time . . . I'm glad you're back."

LES ENFANTS DU PARADIS, 1946

⊚⊚⊚⊚⊚⊚⊚⊚⊚⊚⊚⊚⊚⊚⊚⊚⊚⊚⊚⊚⊚⊚⊚

Les Enfants du Paradis (*The Children of Paradise*) was made by Marcel Carné in France during World War II but not released here until 1946, being held up by censors for reasons too puerile to go into.

The film is a period love story centered around the actors and other "odd" personalities who inhabit a "circus" street in Paris known as "the Boulevard of Crime." The children of paradise of the movie's title are the audiences who sit in a theater's uppermost gallery, or "the gods," where the cheapest seats are located. These are the people the actors love best and play for most heartily.

The heroes of the film are Baptiste, a pantomimic artist, and Garance, the beautiful, mature, sexually desirable woman he loves, played respectively by Jean-Louis Barrault and Arletty. Baptiste misses his chance with Garance at the beginning of this two-and-a-half-hour film (the original was four) because he is too frightened and nervous to go to bed with her. Their romance has blossomed too quickly for him to cope with. And so she becomes mistress to another man, goes away, and Baptiste himself eventually marries. Years pass.

Unknown to Baptiste, Garance returns, reserves a permanent seat at the theater, and watches him perform. Although he has not set eyes on Garance since they first parted, Baptiste, happily married, has nonetheless never forgotten her. And then—*voilà*— they meet!

They spend a night of incredible joy together, but in the morning Baptiste's wife, who has discovered their tryst, confronts the two of them with her children. She clearly loves her husband and does not want to give him up. In this delicately tense confrontation scene, Arletty realizes it would be better for all concerned if she stepped out of the lives of Baptiste and his wife. She bids farewell and departs into the street, where a great festival is in progress. With this action the audience expects Baptiste to reunite with his wife and the film to come to an end, but alas, we are in for a surprise. What follows is a sequence of such magnitude, suspense, frustration, and anguish that it remains years after the first viewing, in my own case over a quarter of a century.

Baptiste looks at his wife and children, but instead of begging forgiveness or attempting some other communication which would have led to a *rapprochement*, he simply tells her that he is really in love with Garance, has always been in love with her, and cannot let her go out of his life now that he has found her again. And so he takes leave of his saddened, astonished wife and children, and rushes into the street to catch up with Garance before she gets too far away from him.

The crowd in the Boulevard of Crime is massive by this time, with people jostling, surging, singing, dancing in festive madness. Streamers fly everywhere; banners swirl and dip; the sound of voices is like the din of cannon fire. Baptiste sees Garance a distance ahead of him and yells to her but she cannot hear him. He pushes and squirms and claws through the crowds, but still she does not hear his voice calling her name. Finally she emerges from the end of the street, enters a coach, gives some instructions to the driver, and, not knowing Baptiste has given up his family for her and is but a short distance behind, drives away.

The camera cuts to a relentless track shot of Baptiste pushing his way through the crowds, calling, "Garance! Garance!" But as he continues his struggle and as he persists in repeating her name, very gradually the camera begins to pull back in a crane shot from its close view of his heaving frame and determined, anxiety-ridden face. We move farther and farther up and back until we find it difficult to discern Baptiste from the hundreds of other faces around him. Nor can we hear the name "Garance!", the din has become so overwhelming.

Finally we are at rooftop level, looking at the gray morning sky, and have lost our hero entirely.

And so the picture ends.

DUEL IN THE SUN, 1946

If there should ever be a place in the halls of cinematic merit for
the "great bad moments of all time," then among the top four or
five positions of indistinction one would surely go to the climax
of David O. Selznick's production of *Duel in the Sun*. Here, in a
grimly barren setting, bad dramatic taste combines with a
garishly ostentatious camera plus mawkish, warped sentiment to
show the destruction of the sick heroine and the depraved outlaw.

Jennifer Jones and Gregory Peck shoot it out over a broad
tumble of boulders and cactus and mortally wound each other.
At this point, realizing the real love they have always borne,
Peck screams that he is dying and Jones starts her epic crawl toward him so that they can expire (perspire would be more appropriate considering the intense heat) in each other's embrace.
That crawl simply has to be seen to be disbelieved. Done in a
mix of oozing blood and dirt, with meticulous close-ups of
Jones's fingers, scratched, torn, and matted, clawing in the desert
terrain, every dreadful nuance of the two-hundred-yard odyssey
is caught on frame.

Finally the two of them are able to clasp bloody hands and
mercifully die, and as the camera draws back for an awesome
crane shot of the expired pair a flower appears where their bodies have been and Orson Welles's narration wraps it all up.

Good grief!

PANIC, 1946

⊙⊛⊙⊛⊙⊛⊙⊛⊙⊛⊙⊛⊙⊛⊙⊛⊙⊛⊙⊛⊙⊛⊙⊛⊙

It is all but forgotten now, but when it was released *Panic*, directed by Julien Duvivier, presented its audiences with one of the most horrifying suspense climaxes since Hitchcock's *Saboteur*. The mise en scène is that of a suburban French slum complete with tall, cramped rooming houses and shabby Bohemian dens.

The hero, Mr. Heer, played by Michel Simon, is a bearded, austere man whose obsession is photography. He holds the proof that Alice's boy friend, Paul, is the murderer of one Audrey Corbet. Alice, a sexy ex-convict portrayed by Viviane Romance, plays up to Heer in order to determine the exact nature of the proof in his possession. She is not successful in her efforts and so she and her boy friend conspire to make the community think that Mr. Heer himself is the murderer. They plant Audrey Corbet's purse in his room and arrange for its discovery, whereupon a band of local citizens surrounds Heer in the street, taunts him, and knocks him down. In panic he flees from the hysterical crowd and seeks refuge among the steep rooftops of the quarter. At one point, in attempting to climb down a slope and into a window, Michel Simon slips, slides down the roof and over the edge, but manages to cling onto the eavestrough.

What then follows are four of the tensest minutes on celluloid. As Heer hangs high above the gathering crowds, the music from a nearby circus forming an ironic background to his terror, his strength slowly diminishes and his face contorts in desperate pain. The camera relentlessly pursues the doomed man from all angles while the eavestrough slowly begins to groan loose from its supports. The circus stops functioning and all is dreadful silence as the camera probes the gaping, awestruck faces of the crowd. Even Alice and Paul stare transfixed at the horror above them. Close-ups of the tortured, sweat-beaded face of the bearded man emphasize his awful distance from the pavement below. The eavestrough creaks again, and sags.

Then, when all hope appears to be lost, we hear fire sirens and, within moments, a tall ladder and a fireman are being propelled upward toward the dangling figure. The fireman is now a few inches from Heer, directly abreast of him. The fireman's calm, confident voice quietly tells the bearded man to reach around and place one hand on the rung of the ladder. The fireman's own arms are reaching out ready to encircle him as he makes this move. Heer makes his decision and removes, painfully, one hand from the eavestrough, half turning his body as he attempts to place it on the ladder. The fireman grasps his waist, but then the worst happens. Heer's hand, weakened from the long minutes spent clamped to the eavestrough, takes hold of the ladder rung but fumbles and slips its grasp. Desperately, Heer swings his other arm around but his movement comes too late. The sheer weight of his body jerks him away from the fireman's clutching grasp and, in an awful hush, he drops five stories to the pavement beneath.

THE BEST YEARS OF OUR LIVES, 1946

⊚⊙⊚⊙⊚⊙⊚⊙⊚⊙⊚⊙⊚⊙⊚⊙⊚⊙⊚⊙⊚

Fredric March dances with his wife, Myrna Loy, in a supper-club in *The Best Years of Our Lives* on the night after his return from four years of separation from her during World War II. Hoagy Carmichael is at the piano, and life is bouncy, dreamy, happy, slightly tipsy. It is one of those moments created by a delicate chemistry of scripting, acting, the direction of William Wyler, and the camerawork of Gregg Toland, not to mention lighting, sound, and all of the other arts and crafts that contribute to the medium. Fredric March proceeds to flirt with his wife, Myrna Loy. One of the genius aspects of the scene is—thanks to novelist MacKinlay Kantor and scriptwriter Robert Sherwood—that he flirts with her *because* she is his wife. The sequence is incredibly carefree and wonderful and is infused with marvelously soul-inspiring élan. Its delicacy of touch is almost Gallic.

GREAT EXPECTATIONS, 1947

Film advertisements back in 1947 informed us that two or three minutes (I forget which) after the beginning of this motion picture we, the audience, could expect the pinnacle shock of our lives. And so we paid our seventy-five cents admission, took our seats, and waited.

It might seem strange that, forewarned as we had been, we still reacted as though a thunderbolt had hit us when the promised "shock" occurred. But we did. We went straight up in the air about ten feet.

The electric moment happens during a long track shot when young Pip (Anthony Wager) is in a cemetery in the dark of evening. He is frightened by a tree creaking in the wind, and starts to run. He runs as though the very devil were after him, the camera relentlessly moving with him, half silhouetting his swift form against a bleak wash of sky as it moves past stunted, gnarled trees and sloping tombstones. Without a moment's hesitation, with no slackening of pace, Pip runs straight into the six-and-a-half-foot frame of the convict Magwich.

Boom!!! David Lean was never more dramatic.

THE RED SHOES, 1948

The art of foreshadowing, of preparing audiences for what is to come, has never been used to greater inverted or ironic effect than in Pressburger and Powell's *The Red Shoes*. This film about a ballet company starred Anton Walbrook, Moira Shearer, and Robert Helpmann.

In the middle of the picture impresario Walbrook is discussing with reporters his plans for a ballet based on the fable of *The Red Shoes*. Attired in a black dressing gown, and carrying a cigarette with affected abandon, he presents an outline of the plot but stops a bit short of the actual ending. One inquiring reporter asks him what happens to the heroine in the end (the part will be played by Moira Shearer when he casts it). Walbrook looks at the man, then turns, shrugging, and tosses away his reply as though it were of no greater significance than the ash on his cigarette. "In the end she dies," he says.

It is only in the end when Moira Shearer is carried to her death by the pair of red shoes that cannot stop dancing that the grim, ironic significance of that "throwaway" becomes apparent.

THE LADY FROM SHANGHAI, 1948

⊚⊙⊚⊙⊚⊙⊚⊙⊚⊙⊚⊙⊚⊙⊚⊙⊚⊙⊚⊙⊚

Everett Sloane and Rita Hayworth shoot it out in front of Orson Welles's amazed Irish eyes in *The Lady from Shanghai,* also directed by Welles, and the screen erupts in a kaleidoscope of smashing glass and fractured images.

The setting is a house of mirrors in a midway, and the motivations are hatred, revenge, and decadence. In fact the entire mood of the film is one of decay and evil. The rest of the movie is interesting and inventive, as are all films by this remarkable motion picture maker, but it is the climax that stands out so boldly, indeed, from most films in the crime drama genre.

The images and fragments of images are fascinating to behold. Rita shreds and chips and cracks and shatters in shards of glass before our eyes and parts of Sloane are broken and exploded as the two demolish each other.

A splendid screen moment.

THE TREASURE
OF THE SIERRA MADRE, 1948

⊚⊚⊚⊚⊚⊚⊚⊚⊚⊚⊚⊚⊚⊚⊚⊚⊚⊚⊚⊚⊚⊚

Near the end of *The Treasure of the Sierra Madre,* John Huston's brilliant treatment of the great adventure novel by B. Traven, our two prospectors, Walter Huston and Tim Holt, find that the gold they have put into bags and hidden under fur pelts tied to their burros has been discovered by a band of nomadic bandits but mistaken for sand, the bags having been hacked open by machete knives and the gold blown away by the wind "back to the hills from whence it came."

The colossal irony of what has just occurred is too much for Old Howard (Huston), who breaks into a toothless laugh which, with Tim Holt's splendid help, mounts to sheer hysteria in a truly incredible screen moment. Huston manages to utter, between bursts, the idea that whatever the trick man or God has played upon them, their entire adventure was worthwhile if only for the story they had to tell.

Earlier in the film our three prospectors (Humphrey Bogart has not yet fallen prey to the wandering bandits) reach the foothills of the Sierra Madre and Huston discovers the first real traces of gold. Huston humorously taunts his two compatriots for not noticing the same mineral signs he had come across and asks them if they have ever beheld bigger fools than themselves (Bogart and Holt actually look at each other in a close two shot following this question). Then Huston laughs maniacally and does a jig the like of which the screen has never witnessed—not until he roars his head off at the end, that is. The moment works brilliantly on its own, and provides a beautiful foreshadowing of the climax.

Walter Huston's performance in this picture happens to be my all-time film favorite.

THE BROTHERS, 1948

@@@@@@@@@@@@@@@@@@@@@@@@@

The Brothers was made in the U.K. by J. Arthur Rank. For sheer sadism, treachery, and violence, it may well be the grimmest film of the forties, and I would include any war film in this comparison.

The fights are unduly savage; there is a sequence in which one of the young Scottish clansmen who dominate the picture gets his thumb caught in a gigantic clam shell just as the tide is starting to come in and must amputate it with his penknife (which he does, about two inches below water level) before the tide can drown him; and then there is the "silver fish and tackle" sequence.

I still emit a groaning shudder when I reflect upon this episode. As a unique form of supposedly retributive revenge, one of the two opposing clans kidnaps the leader of the other clan and, after gagging him so that he cannot utter a sound, the members submerge him in the ocean by buoys and weights so that only his head remains above the surface. To the top of his head is bound, by fishing tackle, a silver fish, so shiny it could be seen for miles. The uninitiated might still puzzle the intention of this curious setup, but only until the seagulls appear in the sky, detect the fish, and start to dive. Then the message becomes horrifyingly clear. In swooping down with their sharp beaks for the silver fish, the birds will slowly shatter the brains of the manacled victim.

THE QUEEN OF SPADES, 1949

⊚⊚⊚⊚⊚⊚⊚⊚⊚⊚⊚⊚⊚⊚⊚⊚⊚⊚⊚⊚⊚⊚

Anton Walbrook stares down at a bier containing a dead woman, Dame Edith Evans. He has driven her to death in an effort to force from her the secret of three cards which, if played in a particular order in faro at the gaming tables, will invariably win. The film is Thorold Dickinson's *The Queen of Spades*, and the mood is grim and macabre.

Walbrook plays a Prussian engineer in eighteenth-century Russia who is possessed by devils in his ruthless, materialistic ambition to "break the bank" of the then famous gambling establishment in St. Petersburg. When he learns that old Dame Edith Evans possesses the "secret of the cards," he stops at nothing to gain entrance to her household, where he uses every device of mental torture at his command to make her reveal this information. But he fails, and the poor woman dies in despair and anguish.

Still determined to wrest the secret from her even in death, he visits her coffin in the cathedral funeral chamber, where torches send up smoke into the dim atmosphere and cast eerie shadows of the mourners on the massive stone walls. Walbrook, feeling he has been cheated, glares down in abject hate at the terribly still face of the dead woman that lies waxen and white before him.

Suddenly she opens her eyes and looks at him.

And that is the moment one can never forget.

In horror Walbrook crosses himself and runs screaming from the premises. Although the rest of the film is marvelously executed, including Walbrook's visitation by the ghost of the dead woman, who reveals to him the "secret of the cards," his last night at the gaming tables, and the ultimate twist of fate that drives him to instant madness, one never forgets the moment when Dame Edith Evans, motionless in death, abruptly opens her eyes.

THE HEIRESS, 1949

◎◎◎◎◎◎◎◎◎◎◎◎◎◎◎◎◎◎◎◎◎

In *The Heiress,* directed by William Wyler, Montgomery Clift thinks that Olivia De Havilland has forgiven him his betrayal. Years earlier he had failed to show up at her doorstep on the night of their planned elopement. Now he has returned and finds that she has matured into a handsome and lovely woman, and he has restated his love for her. He hopes that she has rediscovered her old love for him and will now run away with him. But alas, he is dead, dead wrong.

At the film's climax Catherine Sloper (Olivia) mounts the great hallway staircase of her mansion on Washington Square as Morris Thompson (Clift) pounds on the front door calling her name. Candle in hand, her face bears a look of proud triumph as she rounds a curve in the stairs, leaving her betrayer the way she had once been left—in limbo.

Clift, in a state of frenzy, pounds furiously on the door and continues to pound as "The End" steals up on the screen and the film fades.

THE SET-UP, 1949

⊚⊚⊚⊚⊚⊚⊚⊚⊚⊚⊚⊚⊚⊚⊚⊚⊚⊚⊚⊚⊚⊚

There is no music in *The Set-Up,* Robert Wise's grimly realistic study of the boxing world, and the running time of the film, about ninety minutes, covers exactly the same length of time in the lives of the protagonists. Robert Ryan goes into the ring for sixty or seventy dollars and wins when he is supposed to have "taken a fall." In a moment of awesome violence, one that burns deeply into the memory, he is held down by thugs in an alley and gets his fist pulverized by a brick, all sounds obliterated by a jazz group in an adjoining bar. Wise films the scene in silhouettes against a brick wall, leaving the grisly details to the imagination.

THE BICYCLE THIEF, 1949

At the end of Vittorio De Sica's *The Bicycle Thief* a small boy observes his father being caught by a group of citizens for stealing a bicycle. At the beginning of the film the father has had his own bicycle stolen and, it being the sole means of sustenance for himself and his family in postwar Rome (his job was to put up movie posters of such stars as Rita Hayworth all across the city), he has spent the film trying to track down the thief and get his bicycle back.

Because of his family's poverty he is finally driven to desperation and becomes a bicycle thief himself. But he is caught and, in an agonizing scene, publicly shamed. His little boy moves up behind him and is a witness to his terrible embarrassment and ignominy. Alone, with nowhere to go and no one to turn to, the father simply faces the ridicules and jeers and insults of the crowd that surrounds him. But then his little boy moves close to him and very gently lets his hand steal into his father's to let him know that he is there and with him. The shot of their hands, reminiscent of Charlie Chaplin's *The Kid* (with Jackie Coogan), is timeless cinema.

JOUR DE FÊTE, 1949

One of the great moments of pure visual comedy occurs in Jacques Tati's *Jour de Fête*. The sequence is notable not only for its witty content but because it uses with exceeding skill the screen's special power for depth perspective.

A farmer, leaning on a pitchfork handle, is standing on the brow of a hill, his back very close to the camera. He is looking off down into the background of the shot where a road winds through a small valley. A postman (Tati) is cycling along this road when suddenly he begins to wave his arms wildly above his head. He is being attacked by a bee which we, the audience, naturally cannot see or hear. All we can see are the postman's erratic arm and body movements as he tries to ward off the insect. The farmer, from whose viewpoint we observe the activity, continues his calm, stoical gaze. Finally, in desperation, the postman picks up his bicycle and commences to whirl it around and around in a frantic effort to frighten away the bee. At last he succeeds, mops his brow, mounts his bike, and rides off down the road, disappearing out of the far end of the valley.

Motionless, the farmer follows all of this action. Now everything is still, for the cyclist has gone. Then, suddenly, there is the loud rasp of buzzing close to the camera. Our farmer frantically starts to wave *his* hands and arms and pitchfork over *his* head as the bee selects him for its next target.

GIVE US THIS DAY, 1949

⊚⊚⊚⊚⊚⊚⊚⊚⊚⊚⊚⊚⊚⊚⊚⊚⊚⊚⊚⊚⊚⊚

In *Give Us This Day* director Edward Dmytryk has his hero die under the most agonizing of circumstances, and he stages this scene over the course of a beautiful, sunshine-filled noon hour in downtown Manhattan, with people never far away.

Sam Wanamaker plays an Italian construction worker married to a lovely young girl and just starting to make his way in America. Trapped in a fairly deep wooden "form" which is slowly being filled with fresh, wet concrete, the noise from the cement mixer obscuring his pleading cries, our hero cannot raise any help because his colleagues are all at lunch. And so, in the bright sunshine of a spring afternoon, he suffocates.

Pietro di Donato wrote the novel.

The Fifties

Two developments of the forties, one legal, one technological, came to fruition in this decade and had a disastrous effect upon the motion picture industry.

In the fifties the motion picture companies were finally forced by anti-trust laws to divest themselves of their theater chains across North America and hence lost the powerful and profitable market monopoly they had hitherto enjoyed.

In the fifties television passed through pubescence into manhood in staggeringly quick order and stole away for good the very habit that the film industry had flourished upon; the habit of weekly movie-going.

Despite present-day successes like *The Godfather, Jaws, Star Wars,* and *Close Encounters of the Third Kind,* it is no exaggeration to say that the motion picture industry has never recovered from these blows. Marquee lights began going out by the thousands and bingo became the new starring attraction. Today fewer than one hundred features per annum are made in total by the major companies.

The movies tried to fight back with CinemaScope, VistaVision, Cinerama, Todd-AO, AromaRama, stereophonic sound, and 3-D with glasses for a short time, and lost an intimate innocence in the process. Large screens, offering more for the eye to absorb, slowed down the pacing of films and lengthened scenes, tended to spectacularize even the subtlest of domestic dramas, and took the emphasis away from the human and placed it on the technological. The rhythms produced for smaller screens by the kind of editing I had grown up with were no more, and some of the magic began to disappear from motion pictures.

The rebellion wasn't limited to technology. Marlon Brando and James Dean, in films like *The Wild One* and *Rebel Without a Cause*, attacked a whole status quo way of life in their seemingly less structured "method" style of acting and in their on-screen attitudes toward law and order, the home, love, work, progress. Otto Preminger released *The Moon Is Blue* without the Production Code Administration seal of approval and, together with foreign imports which dealt with sex with greater maturity, helped to usher in a new era in which there was a franker treatment of previously taboo material. And Elvis Presley picked up his guitar, began to shake his hips, and the postwar baby boom had its first messiah.

In Britain, the government ceased to inject large sums into the movie industry as it had in the immediate postwar years, and the bottom quite literally fell out of that film economy. With the exception of a cluster of Alec Guinness comedies like *Kind Hearts and Coronets* (1949), *The Lavender Hill Mob* (1950), and *The Captain's Paradise* (1953), and such Anglo-American co-productions as *The Bridge on the River Kwai* (1957), there was little to compare with the forties.

In France Henri-Georges Clouzot made *The Wages of Fear* (1953) and *Diabolique* (1954), two all-time classics of fear and terror; Japan gave Akira Kurosawa to the world and we marveled at *Rashomon* (1950), *Seven Samurai* (1954), and *Throne of Blood* (1957); India's Satyajit Ray directed the "Apu" trilogy, led by *Pather Panchali* (1954); and Sweden's Ingmar Bergman brought a new language and artistry to the cinema with *Wild Strawberries* (1957) and *The Seventh Seal* (1957).

American movies of the fifties, like Stanley Kramer's production of *High Noon*, reflected changes that had begun to take root in society since World War II. No longer could we feel quite the degree of permanence about the world around us, our lives and institutions, that we had before. We were more skeptical and more cynical. Conflicting values and social stress, as manifested in such phenomena as the cold war and McCarthyism, were indicative of an upheaval that was starting to take place. This upheaval would have to await the coming decade for full blooming because it would be then that the new younger generation, born in the immediate postwar baby boom of the mid to late forties, would come of age.

In the meantime we would be living through an interim, a period of going rather than arriving, and the movies of the time would indicate some of the tensions inherent in this frustrating crossing.

WOMAN ON THE RUN, 1950

⊚⊛⊛⊛⊛⊛⊛⊛⊛⊛⊛⊛⊛⊛⊛⊛⊛⊛⊛⊛⊛⊛⊛

One of the most bizarre thrillers of all time, yet remembered by very few genre aficionados, is an adroit, imaginative little number by Norman Foster called *Woman on the Run*. It was released by Universal-International and starred Ann Sheridan, Dennis O'Keefe, and Robert Keith.

Ann Sheridan searches the streets of San Francisco for her estranged husband, who is the sole observer of the murder of an important trial witness. A reporter, Dennis O'Keefe, anxious for a scoop, secures her confidence and joins her in the hunt. And never far away is detective Robert Keith, who tries to gain Miss Sheridan's help but is constantly rebuffed because she resents police tactics.

During the long search she discovers: (1) that her husband is suffering from a heart disease and will die unless certain medicine is brought to him, (2) that her husband is really very much in love with her, (3) that her faithful friend, Dennis O'Keefe, is really the murderer of the trial witness and wants to kill her husband so that he can never testify.

The climax occurs at night at a bustling amusement park. Sheridan, seated alone and helpless on a cyclone (roller coaster), at last aware of O'Keefe's real intentions, and desperate for the help of Robert Keith, gets momentary flashes through the web of wooden girders of her husband standing on a great floodlit platform in the center of the cyclone pit, and O'Keefe coming to kill him. The flickering images of the two men far below dance and jar through the girders with every movement of the cyclone as it rounds a curve (that's the moment, perhaps three seconds in length), and then the images vanish as she drops, screaming with the other riders, into a dip.

Keith makes it on time.

KIND HEARTS AND CORONETS, 1949

⊚⊚⊚⊚⊚⊚⊚⊚⊚⊚⊚⊚⊚⊚⊚⊚⊚⊚⊚⊚⊚⊚⊚

In Robert Hamer's *Kind Hearts and Coronets* (the movie was, in fact, released in 1949, but to me it belongs in the fifties), set in Victorian England, Dennis Price murders eight members of a family tree, all played by Alec Guinness, in order to achieve an earldom. The deaths are all pretty comic-grisly and without exception are brilliantly executed both by Hamer's ingenious and kinky humor and by Price's and Guinness's performances, but the one that stands out in my mind involves Aunt Agatha (Guinness), who, as an aging suffragette, is sailing over London in a balloon dispensing pamphlets to all and sundry below. Dennis Price has secreted himself in the attic of an old house, and as his aunt passes by he takes deliberate aim with a bow and arrow out of a small window, and fires. We see only Price on the screen at this point and therefore must imagine the grim spectacle before him. As his eyes slowly pan earthward simulating the result of his shot, his voice off screen recites lightly and irreverently:

> "I shot an arrow
> Into the air;
> She fell to earth
> On Berkeley Square."

STRANGERS ON A TRAIN, 1951

⊚◎⊚◎⊚◎⊚◎⊚◎⊚◎⊚◎⊚◎⊚◎⊚◎⊚◎

Farley Granger has the dread feeling that he is being watched as he is driven past a white-pillared Washington museum in Alfred Hitchcock's *Strangers on a Train*—and he is right. Far in the background, as seen from the perspective of Granger's side window by means of a lateral moving camera shot, Robert Walker stands, a dark and ominous shadow, motionless amid a row of marble columns at the top of a broad set of concrete steps. As we move past the museum we keep our focus directly on Walker so that the pillars seem to shift subtly in perspective around him, and yet common sense tells us they can't be moving. The effect is graphically arresting and heightens the mood of the bizarre that shrouds Walker—he is insane and is determined to involve Granger in a plot to murder his wife. Only one shot, but a completely brilliant one.

THE THING, 1951

⊚⊚⊚⊚⊚⊚⊚⊚⊚⊚⊚⊚⊚⊚⊚⊚⊚⊚⊚⊚⊚⊚

An unidentified flying object has arrived from space and landed on a remote ice field in the Arctic. It has buried itself in the snow and ice, which melted because of the heat of the object and subsequently froze solid again.

The Thing, directed by Christian Nyby under Howard Hawks's umbrella, is a dandy piece of science fiction. The great moment occurs after an expeditionary team of scientists has moved in on dog sled to the site of the "landing" and has walked out on the surface of the "lake" to trace the shape of the "object," which they can just barely make out under the ice. The scientists spread out, each one assuming a position immediately above the object's perimeter, then they all raise their heads and look at each other and observe in amazement the pattern their bodies have thus created on the ice surface.

The music is appropriately ominous; the camera pulls back and up and cranes slightly downward upon the group; and what we see before us is a perfect circle.

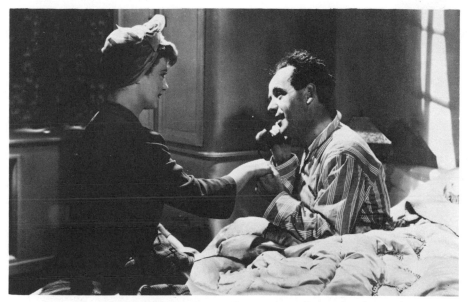

An architect and his wife are invited to a country home for the weekend just before the chilling closing sequence of *Dead of Night*, 1945.

Not the magic moment unhappily, but a scene in which Robert Cummings attracts the attention of some not-too-friendly people in *The Chase*, 1946.

One of many eerie moments in *The Spiral Staircase*, 1946, showing
Dorothy McGuire looking over her shoulder at a nameless presence.

Anthony Wager only has a few seconds to go before running headlong into the sinister Magwich, played by Finlay Currie, in *Great Expectations*, 1947.

Pierre Brasseur (left), Louis Salou, and Albert Remy in a scene from *Les Enfants du Paradis*, 1946.

Tim Holt (left), Humphrey Bogart, and Walter Huston discuss the gold for which they have been searching in *The Treasure of the Sierra Madre*, 1948.

Robert Keith (left) gives Ann Sheridan a morgue's-eye view while Dennis O'Keefe watches with sinister interest in *Woman on the Run*, 1950.

Alec Guinness in one of his eight roles, this time as an amateur photographer, from *Kind Hearts and Coronets,* 1950.

Simone Signoret and Vera Clouzot plot the death by bathtub drowning of a sadistic schoolmaster in *Diabolique,* 1954.

Rock Hudson loses this fight in the diner but wins a moral victory in the magic moment from *Giant*, 1956.

Victor Sjostrom tries to recover his lost youth near his parents' cottage where he spent his childhood summers in *Wild Strawberries*, 1957.

Charlton Heston receives a fatal arrow in battle, but later leads the
victory charge, a dead man roped upright on his horse, near the end of
El Cid, 1961.

Henri Serre (left), Jeanne Moreau, and Oskar Werner are seen here in
a scene from *Jules and Jim*, 1961.

Ron Starr riding a camel outruns the horses in the splendid opening of *Ride the High Country*, 1962.

Ben Johnson, Warren Oates, William Holden, and Ernest Borgnine march to their doom in *The Wild Bunch*, 1969.

AN OUTCAST OF THE ISLANDS, 1952

◉◎◉◎◉◎◉◎◉◎◉◎◉◎◉◎◉◎◉◎◉◎◉

There are two moments in Carol Reed's film of Joseph Conrad's *An Outcast of the Islands* that I want to refer to. Made in England, the picture is set in the Malayan archipelago sometime in the twenties or before and traces the decay and fall from grace of a white man, portrayed magnificently by Trevor Howard.

One moment occurs on the veranda of a plantation house where owner Robert Morley is cuddling his golden-haired little daughter and speaking to her in baby talk. Trevor Howard comes by to ask a favor and Morley doesn't want to be bothered with him, wants to get rid of him, in fact. Without altering the language he is using with his daughter, the pitch of his voice rises in anger and, face perspiring, jowls jiggling, he declares: "Dadda hate bad man! Dadda not like bad man! Dadda want bad man to go away!"

The other moment is the climax, when Howard is left stranded with a beautiful native woman on a jungle island during the rainy season (the woman never speaks throughout the film, incidentally). Howard has betrayed her and she plans to kill him in her own patient time. As Captain Lingar (Ralph Richardson), a man who had once befriended him, sails away from the island in his launch leaving our protagonist behind, Howard is last seen standing on a beach, blinded by the rain, screaming in threatening vengeance: "We'll meet again, Captain Lingar; we'll meet again!"

HIGH NOON, 1952

Gary Cooper walks out onto the deserted main street of Hadleyville, a lone figure, forsaken by all of his fellow citizens, about to face four desperate men who have come to kill him. Cooper looks grimly at his right hand, then stares into the white heat of the day. As the camera takes a long downward crane shot of him, a shot that highlights his utter aloneness against the rooftops of the entire community, the background score strikes its haunting theme and he starts slowly up the street to meet his destiny. So we lead into the wonderfully choreographed gunfight climax of Fred Zinnemann's *High Noon*.

THE WAGES OF FEAR, 1953

Two trucks loaded with cans of nitroglycerine are being driven across three hundred miles of wild Central American terrain. The nitroglycerine is intended to blow up an oil well fire that has gotten out of control. The film is H.-G. Clouzot's *The Wages of Fear*, and the effect on audiences is that of an unrelenting nightmare.

After the characters have been established and the scene set for the journey, the movie embarks upon one horrifying sequence after another. The scene in which the leading truck explodes is ingeniously executed.

It is morning, and in the doomed truck the driver's mate is using the rearview mirror to shave. The driver is singing a song from his homeland, and the mood is cheerful and happy. In the truck a mile behind, Yves Montand is at the wheel while Charles Vanel, beside him, is beginning to roll a cigarette. Quite suddenly, in a huge close-up, we see the tobacco being sucked right out of the half-rolled paper. Next we observe two dull flashes of light reflected in Vanel's face as he looks up and out the window ahead of him. Then we see what he sees, a giant column of smoke emerging over the horizon accompanied by a heavy, rumbling explosion.

Later, when Vanel and Montand reach the site of the tragedy, nothing remains except two roadside lines of bleached tree boles shorn of their bark and all their upper limbs, and a two-hundred-yard pool of oil caused by a break in the pipeline flanking the road. Within minutes, however, the two men are plunged into another grisly episode which takes one of their lives.

Because it would only take a slight jar from an unseen stone under the wheel of the truck to set off the entire cargo, Charles Vanel wades through the enormous pool of oil covering the roadbed—he is about fifty feet in front of the slowly moving truck—to detect any invisible obstructions hidden below the black surface. At one point he pauses and bends down to remove a tree branch when, abruptly, the pinned limb, anchored at one end by some obscured obstacle, springs out of the oil, slaps Vanel across his midriff, and sends his off-balanced body down into the pool, clamping it in a desperate position, as the next few moments are about to reveal.

Held in an awkward sitting angle, his body from the waist downward moored below the oil surface by the tree branch in such a way, judging by the terror that mounts on his grease-stained face, that one of his legs projects across the path of one of the wheels of the ominously moving truck, Vanel waits in horror for the giant, rotating tire to pass over him. He knows that Montand cannot stop the truck on such short notice without risking a fatal shudder to the volatile nitroglycerine. And so a wheel, oil dripping from its moving, corrugated surface, passes within inches of the man's screaming face.

Earlier in this film, there is a sequence in which our four heroes must blow up a huge boulder which is blocking their way. They don't have dynamite, but they *do* have a very potent explosive with them, and so they drill a narrow, vertical hole down into the upper surface of the rock and—you had better hold onto something when you hear this—proceed to fill it, drop by drop, with nitroglycerine.

This scene ranks with the greatest suspense moments of the silver screen. A willow wand has been shaved and dipped into a thermos bottle of the water-clear nitro so that, during the procedure to follow, drops will cling to its pre-moistened surface. Then the wand is inserted into the hole and the mouth of the thermos bottle is tilted against the wand's glistening stem. The camera cuts sadistically from close-up to close-up of the tension-riven faces of the four men as the drops of nitroglycerine sparkle in the sun and disappear down the wand into the hole.

They ignite their explosive device by tying a short hammer with a length of fuse to an improvised tepee of sticks over the mouth of the hole that contains the nitro. Then they run a long fuse away from this contraption and, once they are all safely concealed behind a hill, ignite it. The fuse burns, the hammer drops onto the surface of the hole, and a whale of an explosion follows.

But there is a consequence.

High up on the slope of a flanking hill the explosion dislodges a boulder. Charles Vanel, seated in the cab of his truck, its door open, becomes grimly fascinated by the downward progress of the boulder. And as its bounds become greater he realizes that he and the truck are directly in the boulder's path. Vanel starts to shake, his whole body vibrating in terror. The rock hits a few yards from the truck, then bounces right over him. Vanel staggers to a ditch and vomits.

THE CAPTAIN'S PARADISE, 1953

◎◎◎◎◎◎◎◎◎◎◎◎◎◎◎◎◎◎◎◎◎

The opening of Ealing Studios' production of *The Captain's Paradise* is an outrageous, cliff-hanging sequence in which Alec Guinness is marched up a hill and stood before a firing squad in a Moroccan courtyard. As the camera cuts to an exterior view of the courtyard showing vultures circling expectantly above the surrounding ramparts, he is *shot*—at least we hear the officer in charge of the execution shouting his instructions and we hear all the rifles go off so we know he *must* have been shot. And we thank the director for sparing us the grisly details.

Next we flash back over Guinness's life as a ferry boat captain who plies the waters between Gibraltar and Morocco and who is the happy, bigamous possessor of a wife in each port. Inasmuch as the two wives (Celia Johnson and Yvonne De Carlo) are entirely different in personality attributes and in physical make-up, they each satisfy strong and distinct needs within Guinness. Hence, in conjunction with the ferry boat, whose name happens to be *The Golden Fleece*, they comprise the "paradise" of the title.

In the end Guinness's utopia backfires on him when the two women begin to switch roles, something he cannot psychologically cope with. Up until this point he has been able to keep his little world running harmoniously. He has been able to overcome all problems because he seems to have an incredible genius for overcoming all problems and getting what he wants. A chain reaction ensues, and before he knows what is happening he finds himself indicted for a crime (the death of Yvonne De Carlo) that he did not commit.

And so the picture ends where it began, with Guinness being marched up a hill toward his doom.

The same footage is repeated. Our hero stands very still before the firing squad, and closes his eyes; the guns are raised, the fatal command is given, and as we move in for a close-up of Guinness, the guns are fired.

We do not cut to an exterior of the courtyard this time and, therefore, we wait to see our captain collapse before our eyes.

But he doesn't collapse.

He simply stands quite silently and, in a splendid moment of cinematic surprise, opens his eyes.

A smile breaks across his lips. He reaches into a pocket, produces a thick wad of money, and approaches the firing squad, whose rifles are all aimed in the direction of the dead body of the officer in charge of the execution. He walks down the length of the squad paying off each member as he goes. Then he dashes up to the open entrance of the courtyard and stands for a brief moment before departing, looking back toward us, pondering what his next step is going to be. The End.

ESCAPE FROM FORT BRAVO, 1953

William Holden, Eleanor Parker, and others are trapped in a small arroyo, or gully, surrounded by Apaches in *Escape from Fort Bravo*, directed by John Sturges, with seemingly no hope of survival. What makes for fascinating screen viewing is the method the Apaches choose to eradicate our intrepid heroes.

Several braves ride up from different directions and plant spears with tassels on the ends of them on all sides of the trapped group. It doesn't take long for our doomed party to realize that the spears actually form a circle—like the bull's-eye on a dart board—and only a little longer to determine the reason for this.

Apache archers gather some distance away in a tight band, raise their bows to a particular elevation, and fire. Arrows rise in a high arc-like swarm and descend into the gully where Holden's party lies huddled. Only a few arrows make their mark, thus the Apaches correct their elevation and send a second swarm of arrows up, over, and down into the gully. The flight of the arrows is effectively captured by the camera, but the sound man must take a salute here for eerie effects of hum and whine that are shattering to the nervous system.

THE WAR OF THE WORLDS, 1953

In *The War of the Worlds*, directed by Byron Haskin, Gene Barry and Ann Robinson find themselves in a small cottage while all around them, unseen by the camera, Martians are landing. Suddenly we see a glass "eye" at the end of a vacuum-like tube peering in at the room from the open window. By this time Barry and Robinson have secreted themselves behind furniture where, in tense terror, they perspire and wait, hoping the "eye" will not find their location. The "eye" looks around for a few moments and then, like a giant South American anaconda, slides some of the length of its tubing over the sill and glides down into the room. The "snake" slithers this way and that across the room looking behind chairs and chesterfields for its prey. Barry and Robinson by now are almost unable to breathe. The mechanical creature is finally unsuccessful and slips back out the window.

THE BIG HEAT, 1953

⊚⊚⊚⊚⊚⊚⊚⊚⊚⊚⊚⊚⊚⊚⊚⊚⊚⊚⊚⊚⊚

Glenn Ford portrays a tough detective embroiled in a big-city crime in Fritz Lang's *The Big Heat*. The baddies try to buy him off his investigations, but Ford, in the tradition of Dashiell Hammett's heroes, is a law and code unto himself. He refuses to deviate from the object of his pursuit or to abandon his chosen methods. He is determined to round up every last one of the villains and to do so with force if necessary.

During the first twenty minutes of the film, the warm, extraordinarily human relationship between Ford and his wife is developed, and this forms an excellent real-life counterpoint for the murky world of crime into which Ford plummets himself. Then, without any warning whatever, as Ford's wife puts her foot on the starter of his car one evening, the machine explodes, killing her instantly. The way Lang handles her sudden and horrible death so affects us that we endorse every brutality and ruthlessness that Ford adopts in order to see the murderers brought to justice. Although the idea has been employed a good deal since 1953 in an increasing number of vigilante-styled motion pictures, I cannot recall a more powerful motivation for revenge ever impressed upon an audience.

Another grim, grim moment takes place when sadist Lee Marvin tosses a Silex of boiling coffee into Gloria Grahame's face. Again, we are made to feel a hate that knows no bounds.

SHANE, 1953

Elisha Cook, Jr., dies with great élan in *Shane*, George Stevens' epic Western. He is shot down by Jack Palance on the muddy main street of a frontier cow town so primitive it has buildings along only one side. Cook's whole body doubles up in the middle and he leaps violently backward before crumbling into the dirt, thus creating the illusion of two forty-five slugs smacking into his stomach like a baseball bat, which I am told is a quite accurate simile. This is not very pleasant stuff, but in the myth land of the Western it is an absolutely perfect effect.

ON THE WATERFRONT, 1954

◎◎◎◎◎◎◎◎◎◎◎◎◎◎◎◎◎◎◎◎◎◎◎

The moment in *On the Waterfront*, the Academy Award winner by Elia Kazan, that I will never forget—and the film has many memorable sequences, including the famous car scene between the two brothers, Marlon Brando and Rod Steiger, over the possession of a gun—is really a single shot of Brando's face.

The sequence is a touching exchange between the two lovers, Brando and Eva Marie Saint, and the setting is along a simple high chain-link fence. Eva wants Brando to take her with him but knows no real way to communicate this to him. As Brando walks away from her, slowly, we think he does not understand the longing within her and that he is going to leave her behind. Then he pauses, partly turns, looks at the girl, lets his eyes glance obliquely away from her while his face is still directed toward her, and does something with his head, a sort of half nod that tells her everything she wants to know.

The gesture, the expression are a genius of simplicity and our souls rejoice.

HOBSON'S CHOICE, 1954

⊚⊚⊚⊚⊚⊚⊚⊚⊚⊚⊚⊚⊚⊚⊚⊚⊚⊚⊚⊚⊚⊚⊚⊚

Charles Laughton gets drunk quite regularly at a pub called Moonraker's in *Hobson's Choice*, directed by David Lean. In one fine sequence he makes his way home through the dark cobblestone streets by following, and dancing in, a succession of rain puddles, each one carrying a bright reflection of the moon. It is as though the ample figure of Laughton, full of spirit and hilarity, were dancing on the very moonbeams themselves.

TWENTY THOUSAND LEAGUES
UNDER THE SEA, 1954

Walt Disney's screen treatment of Jules Verne's *Twenty Thousand Leagues Under the Sea* is pure movie magic, capturing all of the novel's old-fashioned Victorian science fiction with fidelity and imagination. There are many wonders in this delicious film, not the least of which is the awesome fight with the giant squid at film's end, tentacles reaching down into the very passageways of the submarine, challenging the limits of Kirk Douglas's strength and ingenuity.

But the moment that will always last in my memory is the sequence in which the crew members of the *Nautilus*, Captain Nemo's (James Mason) incredible underwater craft, are depicted returning to the ship with their underwater harvest. Filmed in muted browns and sepias, the scene shows a cluster of men attired in strange diving suits moving along a stretch of sea bottom in a slow-motion, half-inclined attitude, drawing long nets of snails and other sea goodies behind them. It is an amazingly haunting moment that sums up the entire world of Jules Verne, a poetic glimpse of pure wonder.

DIABOLIQUE, 1954

⊚⊚⊚⊚⊚⊚⊚⊚⊚⊚⊚⊚⊚⊚⊚⊚⊚⊚⊚⊚⊚

A miserable, somewhat sadistic schoolmaster, who presides over a boys' school in rural France, is drowned in a bathtub by his wife and his mistress. When the bathtub is emptied the morning following the murder, the camera shot down between the dead man's boots toward the drain is worthy of special mention. It is accompanied by the sucking, rasping sound of the water going out. That night the two ladies (Simone Signoret plays the mistress and Vera Clouzot, the wife) douse the dead man's body with alcohol and drop him into the old slime-surfaced swimming pool at the back of the school. Then, two days later, under the pretext that a wallet has fallen into the same pool, they drain it so that the body can be discovered and a logical explanation given (stumbled while drunk) for the husband's disappearance. Now begin four great moments, one building upon the other until a total frenzy is achieved by director H.-G. Clouzot. The film's title, *Diabolique*, is grandly realized.

First, when the pool is drained, there is no body at its bottom. The wife, who happens to have a bad heart anyway, almost succumbs. The mistress seems made of sterner stuff, and grimly faces that which appears inexplicable.

Second, a few days later, the suit the husband was drowned in is brought to the school by the local cleaners.

Third, when the annual class picture is taken on the steps of the school, all the students having been lined up in neat rows for the shot, and developed in a portable darkroom at the rear of the photographer's van, what should be seen peering from an upstairs window but the face of the dead headmaster.

And fourth, left alone in the school over a holiday weekend, the wife wakes up in the middle of the night and sees, across the quadrangle, the shadow of her dead husband pacing back and forth behind the drawn shades of his study. She bravely goes to investigate, her housecoat clasped tightly around her, the sounds of her husband's typewriter clattering down the long, dark corridor as she advances toward the slit of light streaking from the bottom of his study door. Ultimately she reaches the door, opens it, and discovers his typewriter with a pair of empty gloves sitting on the keys as though they were in the act of typing. On the roll on a sheet of paper is a brief message for her from "beyond." This breaks her, and she runs screaming back to her bathroom for her pills. She can feel another attack coming on. As she fumbles desperately for the pills in her wall cabinet, she happens to cast her eyes toward her bathtub, and there, greeting her, is the floating corpse of her "dead" husband much as he was the night he was "drowned."

This is the proverbial straw that broke the camel's back. Yelling in abject terror, the wife slides down her bathroom wall to the floor and dies of shock. When she is clearly dead, the camera gently pans over to the bathtub for the screen "twist" to end them all.

There, as still as death, floats the body of the dead woman's husband. But not for long. A hand rises out of the water and clasps onto one side of the tub. The other hand does the same. Slowly, very slowly, the "dead man" sits erect, then reaches up and removes contact lenses from each eye, white lenses used to create the illusion of pupils rolled backward. As he steps from the tub he calls to someone in the next room, "Come on in, honey. Well, we did it this time. We really scared the old girl." And in walks mistress Simone Signoret.

THE NIGHT HOLDS TERROR, 1955

⊚⊚⊚⊚⊚⊚⊚⊚⊚⊚⊚⊚⊚⊚⊚⊚⊚⊚⊚⊚⊚⊚⊚⊚

Special tribute should be paid in these pages to the most underrated master of suspense in the history of films, Andrew L. Stone.
In movies like *Julie*, *Cry Terror*, *The Steel Trap*, *The Last Voyage*, and *The Decks Ran Red*, he thrills us again and again in sequences of diabolical contrivance, geared to carry us well beyond the point of collapse, yet usually filmed on location and
with a rigorously detailed sense of realism. *The Night Holds
Terror* affords one exceedingly brilliant example of the Stone
touch.

The plot revolves around a trio of young thugs led by a sadistic criminal, John Cassavetes, who holds Jack Kelly and his family prisoner. The key scene details the efforts of the police to find
where the kidnappers are hiding. They know that a call will be
coming through from Cassavetes at a certain hour and accord-
ingly alert their telephone exchange to be on the ready to trace
the call. But a trace of this kind requires time, therefore the thug
leader has to be delayed while on the phone. This one scene,
with a telephone engineer whirling up and down corridors past
banks of electrical circuitry, at times working on his feet with a
flashlight to check wires, at other times climbing and riding a
ladder that runs on rails along the circuitry passageways to make
similar checks, becomes excruciating as Cassavetes starts to suspect he is being "stalled" while only a few more seconds are
needed by the engineer to track the last two digits.

GIANT, 1956

⊚⊚⊚⊚⊚⊚⊚⊚⊚⊚⊚⊚⊚⊚⊚⊚⊚⊚⊚⊚⊚⊚⊚⊚

The fight in the diner near the end of *Giant,* a production by George Stevens, is a most memorable scene. Rock Hudson, a Texas cattleman turned oilman and a symbol of frontier society, has no sympathy for the sissy concept that a man is his brother's keeper or the idea that all men are created equal. Consequently he has never understood his wife's (Elizabeth Taylor) work toward a more racially just community. And yet, she has finally had some modicum of influence upon him, because when the diner owner tries to oust a poor Mexican and his family from the premises, Hudson takes exception. The fight that ensues is confined to narrow quarters, but it is one of Hollywood's best: hard, fierce, and tinged with humor, yet making its meaning felt every punch of the way. Early in the scuffle Hudson gets banged into the Wurlitzer, and on comes "The Yellow Rose of Texas," which proceeds to extol in rousing fashion the many virtues of the wealthy state while the fight proceeds in the foreground. Finally, Hudson gets knocked onto a table of salad plates, is "out," and loses the fight, but his wife has never been prouder of him than she is at this moment of masculine defeat.

FORBIDDEN PLANET, 1956

⊚⊚⊚⊚⊚⊚⊚⊚⊚⊚⊚⊚⊚⊚⊚⊚⊚⊚⊚⊚⊚⊚⊚⊚

Far in the future on another world millions of light-years distant, human beings wage a war against the monster of the id, an incarnation of the beast that lives deep in all of us. Directed by Fred McLeod Wilcox, *Forbidden Planet* is an imaginatively made, quite spectacular feat of science fictioning that features Walter Pidgeon, Anne Francis, Leslie Nielsen, and Warren Stevens. But the moment I remember is the sequence in which our intrepid heroes come face to face with the beast they have been trying to destroy. This is the first and only time they are able to see it (it goes through the film in a state of invisibility because it represents the collective unconscious or that part of our brain that extends back to elemental, primitive times when hunger, death, and survival dominated). The hunters are finally able to trap it in an electromagnetic field. And there it is, taller than the treetops and bestial beyond one's imagining. Its wild, horrifically animated face and form haunt me to this day.

WILD STRAWBERRIES, 1957

◎◉◈◉◈◉◈◉◈◉◈◉◈◉◈◉◈◉◈◉◈◉◎

My favorite of Ingmar Bergman's films is *Wild Strawberries*. Through flashbacks that permit a complicated and brilliant handling of time, the film details events that occur during a single day's motor trip undertaken by an aging physician. These events frequently take place in the mind of the old doctor, who is soon to be honored for his lifelong contributions to medicine. Three of cinema's greatest, most magical moments occur in this remarkably made and moving film.

In the first, the doctor has a nightmare (Victor Sjostrom is our star) during the early hours of the morning preceding his trip. In it he finds himself on a bright, white, sunlit street near a town hall with a clock that has no hands. A horse-drawn hearse clatters past; one of its huge, spoked wheels rolls loose; and a large, black coffin slides off into the center of the street. The lid of the coffin has become slightly ajar and a rigid hand is protruding into the sunlight. Hypnotized by this hand, the doctor moves slowly but irresistibly toward it. When he reaches the coffin and stares transfixed at the dead fingers, the hand suddenly grabs his arm, the lid slides back, and the doctor finds himself staring down in mute horror at—himself.

In the second, the doctor visits his family's summer home by a lake where he spent much of his youth. He encounters the beautiful girl (Bibi Andersson) his brother loved, who is also the girl *he* desperately loved, kneeling in some grass picking wild strawberries. But rather than leave this scene as one of pure spectator memory, Bergman does an astonishing thing. He has the doctor (old, white-haired) speak to the lovely girl, take her hand, and walk with her through the long grass, the trees, and the warm summer sunlight. The image of the two of them, the old man and the young woman, creates a unique time fusion which, within the story context of the doctor's lost dreams, haunts the viewer's memory.

The third moment comes at the conclusion of the film, as the doctor is about to go to sleep. It is the end of a long day in which he has been beset by guilts and self-doubts and remorse. He allows his mind (for the pleasure it will give him, his off-screen voice informs us) to return once more to the summer home of his youth. There, in the distance, on a rocky point of land on a beautiful day seventy years in the past, he sees his mother and father sitting by the water fishing. They are in suitably white, turn-of-the-century attire, and look altogether charming. The doctor, his aged face warm in expectation, waves to the two of them and, from the distance, across time, his mother and father wave back to him. The expression on Victor Sjostrom's old, craggy but still handsome face, displayed in a long, sunlit close-up, carries such love and feeling that it is almost unbearable to watch. A quick cut to a shot of the doctor turning over in his bed to go to sleep, and the film ends.

The above shot, along with Chaplin's face at the end of *City Lights,* and Walter Huston's in the climax of *The Treasure of the Sierra Madre,* is, in my opinion, one of the three greatest close-ups ever taken.

THE INCREDIBLE SHRINKING MAN, 1957

In an early scene of Jack Arnold's *The Incredible Shrinking Man,* the diminutive hero is given a doll's house to live in by his grief-stricken wife. The tiny abode sits on the living-room floor of the home our hero lived in quite normally. But scant days before, a brush with atomic dust on a yachting jaunt had begun to work its terrible reversal effects upon his growth metabolism.

The episode that still causes me to shudder occurs when the family cat eludes the watchful eyes of the wife and gets inside the house. Prowling the wall-to-wall carpeting with the restless movements of a wild tiger, the cat spies the miniature house and creeps up upon it. We cut inside and observe our hero seated on a sofa contemplating his grim fate. Then, through the toy window over his shoulder, we observe the gigantic blown-up face of the cat peering in at him. The relativity effect is staggering. Our hero tries to back away but seems riveted in terror to the spot. Then a long paw comes in the door feeling for him. . . .

THE BRIDGE ON THE RIVER KWAI, 1957

When British Army officer Colonel Nicholson, played by Alec Guinness, is released from a small tin hut (he has been confined there by Japanese camp commander Sessue Hayakawa) where he has baked for a few days under the Burmese sun, he will not allow anyone to help him but insists on managing, though he is near collapse, on his own strength. The way Guinness staggers across the compound—his bulldog determination and crazed ego, which formerly infuriated us but which we now realize are the mainstays of his survival, showing through every inch of his parched khaki—brings great cheers of triumph from every English prisoner in the camp. The down-angle crane shot of Guinness' weaving figure being surrounded from all sides by a rush of wildly ecstatic soldiers—in the fashion, almost, of an ancient cinematic "iris close"—is a miracle of dignity, insanity, and human survival. The picture, of course, is David Lean's *The Bridge on the River Kwai*.

BEN HUR, 1959

⊚⊚⊚⊚⊚⊚⊚⊚⊚⊚⊚⊚⊚⊚⊚⊚⊚⊚⊚⊚⊚⊚⊚

The chariot race in *Ben Hur* is still one of the most exciting action scenes ever filmed. Around and around the great stone idols in the center of the racing arena, Ben Hur and his archenemy, Messala, duel it out over eight screen minutes to a bitterly grim finale. Ben Hur lives but Messala is a bloody pulp after being dragged under the chopping hooves of horses when his chariot goes to pieces. The pacing and cutting are frenetic in second-unit-director Yakima Canutt's hands. Under the over-all control of director William Wyler, the film starred Charlton Heston and Stephen Boyd.

The Sixties

It was in this decade that the postwar babies came of age and the youth cult came into its own. This was the age of student sit-ins and campus strikes, of urban riots and tragic political assassinations. The seeds of unrest and revolt sown among the conflicting values of the postwar decade bore fruit in the sixties, as reflected in such landmark films as *Easy Rider*, *Bonnie and Clyde*, and *The Wild Bunch*. Sexual taboos, loosened during the fifties, were now wildly thrown aside and the screen enjoyed an unprecedented freedom, as seen in such films as *The Graduate*. The motion picture industry continued to suffer from the competition of television, but lashed back with epics like *Lawrence of Arabia*, *Doctor Zhivago*, and *2001: A Space Odyssey*.

While the British film industry was still virtually crippled in a film production sense—notable exceptions to this statement would include the James Bond movies—the Canadian film industry subsisted mainly on the fine works of the National Film Board and received a strong shot in the arm through the creation of the Canadian Film Development Corporation in 1968, an institution designed to stimulate commercial production by matching private dollars with government dollars in film investment.

But if there was anything that could be termed a flowering during this period it was the French film industry, which bequeathed to the world a cinematic movement known as the *Nouvelle Vague* or New Wave. Here, for the first time, men and women raised on a diet of motion pictures since birth now began to make movies. François Truffaut, Jean-Luc Godard, and Alain Resnais are among the most notable. Attention was drawn as never quite before to the "foreign" film: Ingmar Bergman in Sweden, Akira Kurosawa in Japan, Satyajit Ray in India were several of many international film makers whose works began appearing in North American film houses with even greater regularity than in the fifties.

We are still too close to the sixties to objectively evaluate the decade, but we can say that while large screens seemed to be here to stay, the work of the New Wave, and of Bergman and others, at least indicated an attempt to return the medium to a more intimate mode even if their creations rarely got beyond that slender string of cinemas across the United States and Canada called the "art houses." And certainly such film devices as the jump cut and freeze frame, which the New Wave utilized, were quickly adopted by the major film producers as part of the standard techniques of film making.

THE FACTS OF LIFE, 1960

⊙⊙⊙⊙⊙⊙⊙⊙⊙⊙⊙⊙⊙⊙⊙⊙⊙⊙⊙⊙⊙⊙⊙

Bob Hope and Lucille Ball are each married to other partners in *The Facts of Life* but in the course of the film's early plot developments find themselves at a resort alone together without their spouses. Straight specimens of a very middle middle-classery, the two nonetheless fall in love with each other and launch an affair, but not without trepidations.

The key scene—and one which is probably the high-water mark in the "comedy of frustration"—occurs in (I believe) Las Vegas at night. Hope and Ball have checked into a motel somewhere along a long strip of motels. They are truly looking forward to their night together and are as excited as any middle-aged newlyweds could ever be. But Hope has to drive out to a drugstore to pick up something. He tells Ball he won't be long. He drives possibly a mile or two along the strip to find a store, makes his purchase, then, all a-beam with the expectancy of shortly being with the girl he loves (if memory serves me this would be their first complete night together, earlier attempts having been frustrated by one thing or another), he starts back along the strip. Motels and eating places and night clubs and more motels all glide by in a constant neon montage. Hundreds of motels pass by. Then something stark and terrifying begins to dawn on Bob Hope's face: *he can't remember the name of the motel where he booked in with Lucille Ball!* In desperation he starts to drive frenziedly back and forth along the strip staring at this motel and that one, trying to achieve some glimmer of recognition. He eventually succeeds, but not before the night is consumed.

EL CID, 1961

＠＠＠＠＠＠＠＠＠＠＠＠＠＠＠＠＠＠＠＠＠＠

At the end of *El Cid,* Anthony Mann's splendid adventure-spectacle (possibly the best adventure-spectacle ever made), the body of the dead Spanish leader, played by Charlton Heston, is propped up in the saddle of his horse and sent off into battle at the head of his troops. That scene, a battle charge led by a dead man, carries an awesomeness, a grandeur, that surpasses any scene in other films of this genre. The moving camerawork, the music score, the setting, the costumes, the production values, the brilliant Spanish weather, and a superb performance by Heston conspire under Mann's sensitive hand to make a magnificent moment.

THE GUNS OF NAVARONE, 1961

Director J. Lee Thompson and writer Carl Foreman reward us quite handsomely at the finish of *The Guns of Navarone,* one of the greatest of all adventure films, with enough high-class, slap-bang action for a dozen motion pictures.

Set mostly on a small, German-held island off mainland Greece during some dark days of World War II, the main thread of the tale concerns a tiny group of British-originated commandos. They land on the island with the nigh impossible mission of locating and destroying a massive pair of long-range guns before they can be used against a British fleet due to pass nearby in a matter of days. The reason for the fleet's deployment in that area at that time relates to the evacuation of refugees from another island before it is destroyed.

Heroes Gregory Peck, David Niven, and Anthony Quinn are eminently successful in their grim task, but it is the shot of the great guns toppling from their high, rocky perch into the sea that excites our imaginations. Dynamited from their concrete moorings, the two guns go to their joint doom with exceeding grace, their long, silver shafts glinting majestically as they glide off their buttresses and fall in a slow end-over-end movement into the ocean beneath. The moment has about it an epic awesomeness that has more to do with Homer than Hitler, and with the death of the guns this mood is summed up superbly.

JULES AND JIM, 1961

◎⊚◎⊚◎⊚◎⊚◎⊚◎⊚◎⊚◎⊚◎⊚◎⊚◎⊚◎⊚◎⊚

The ending of *Jules and Jim*, François Truffaut's masterpiece, contains an uncanny passage of harsh reality which becomes a fine counterpoint to the essentially romantic theme of the bulk of the picture.

Catherine is a woman who wants to live as a free soul, scorning conventional morality, in the Bohemian days of pre-World War I Paris. She meets and has high times with Jules, a German, and Jim, a Frenchman. She marries Jules; the war puts the men on opposite sides; then peace comes, Jim pays a visit to the pair, and before we can blink a ménage à trois is being set up before our eyes.

Catherine is a sort of ultimate woman whose presence completely dominates both men, but when she takes other lovers a cloud of rivalry and uncertainty overcomes the paradise that has been created. Catherine becomes disenchanted with Jules, and the two men have a falling-out.

Near the end Catherine takes Jim for a car ride and sails right out over the end of an aqueduct, committing suicide and killing Jim with grand aplomb.

Jules, alone and friendless at the film's close, waits until Catherine's cremation is complete. The beautiful body of the woman he loves is transformed almost before our eyes under blast furnace heat from that of a femme fatale into ashes and bits of gold toothing. These are put into a tiny box which Jules places under his arm. He then walks off. As he moves down a narrow side street away from us to an uncertain future, a lively, haunting carousel-type musical score starts up, swells, and accompanies him into the fade-out. The carousel music romantically recalls Catherine to our memories and hits a brilliant contrast to the preceding scene.

Jeanne Moreau and Oskar Werner star. Henri Serre is Jim.

LAWRENCE OF ARABIA, 1962

⊚⊙⊚⊙⊚⊙⊚⊙⊚⊙⊚⊙⊚⊙⊚⊙⊚⊙⊚⊙⊚⊙⊚⊙⊚

After successfully derailing an enemy train, Peter O'Toole—the picture is *Lawrence of Arabia*—disports himself in his sandals and long, flowing robes along the roof of the wrecked freight cars. This is a scene of great triumph, of unbridled egomania, of charisma and style caught to perfection in a long, moving camera shot which tracks to the accompaniment of Maurice Jarre's stirring score. It is in this kind of grandiloquent irony that director David Lean excels.

RIDE THE HIGH COUNTRY, 1962

⊚⊚⊚⊚⊚⊚⊚⊚⊚⊚⊚⊚⊚⊚⊚⊚⊚⊚⊚⊚⊚⊚

The wedding scene in Sam Peckinpah's *Ride the High Country* is astonishing in its location, a whorehouse in a mining town somewhere along the old frontier. The bridesmaids are all whores, large, grotesque, coarse, no real good-lookers amid the lot, and the plain-timbered room bears the sudden, temporary look of all boom towns, the look of having been assembled overnight.

Edgar Buchanan is the alcoholic J.P. and the dubious wedding partners are Mariette Hartley and James Drury. Hartley is milk-and-corn-fed, wholesome and lovely, no longer in love with the man she has traveled to the gold fields to marry. And no wonder. Drury is a wild, lascivious, hillbilly type who is under the crude domination of a father and siblings, as wild a bunch as we have ever seen guzzle whiskey, whoop, holler, and carouse across a silver screen. While Hartley deplores her husband-to-be—she by now prefers the shy, somewhat sensitive young man (Ronald Starr) who has accompanied her and her two guides (Joel McCrea and Randolph Scott) on the long ride to the mining town—Drury, now that he has cast eyes upon the ripeness of the young lady, cannot wait for the marriage bonds to be tied so that he can wreak his lecherous desires upon her.

The marriage ceremony begins and Edgar Buchanan starts to speak, and when he does one of the golden moments of cinema occurs. For in his brief sermon, delivered in a style of inebriation that suggests not a bender but the state of a man who simply lives with whiskey day and night, Buchanan demolishes forever any romantic notions about the real meaning of marriage. He speaks about long years together—and he emphasizes *long* and

209

catches a most perceptive time sense by his pacing and low-timbred projection—and he speaks about the real implications of partnership and what a vastly different phenomenon this contract is from the freedom and self-concern of the single life. Finally, he winds up on a note capturing the sheer *hardness* of married life. His last words in fact are, "It is hard . . . hard."

Clearly, by his definition, if one is seeking pure comfort and pleasure above all things during this life, one errs if one seeks to find this path in true marriage. Marriage is other things, undeniably fine and rewarding things, but not "romantic" things in the traditional sense of that word.

The ceremony over, Drury prepares to spend his wedding night with his bride in the whorehouse. But other events gain momentum, and the plot surges forward.

Ride the High Country may well be the most lyrical Western ever made; certainly it is one of my favorites. From the crazy race at the opening between a camel and a horse (the camel wins), through the long, delicious dialogues between Scott and McCrea in which romantic memories are counterpointed by the sheer fact that our two heroes are simply growing old (need of glasses to read by, back pains after a ride, etc.), right up to the climactic and tragic gunfight when our two heroes momentarily recapture some of their vanished glory, the picture is in the sure, sensitive control of a fine film maker.

TOM JONES, 1963

⊚⊚⊚⊚⊚⊚⊚⊚⊚⊚⊚⊚⊚⊚⊚⊚⊚⊚⊚⊚⊚⊚⊚

Sexual fulfillment has never found a greater comic metaphor than in the food-orgy scene in Tony Richardson's *Tom Jones*. Albert Finney and Joyce Redman ogle each other while swallowing oysters, ravaging chicken legs, sucking at lobster, and gobbling fruit in an extraordinary parody of love-making.

ZORBA THE GREEK, 1964

⊚⊙⊚⊙⊚⊙⊚⊙⊚⊙⊚⊙⊚⊙⊚⊙⊚⊙⊚⊙⊚⊙

"Zorba, teach me how to dance," says Alan Bates at the end of *Zorba the Greek*, and Anthony Quinn does just that. As a natural descendant on earth of the god Pan, whose soul was wild and free and full of bounteous life, Zorba stretches out his arms at shoulder level to either side and, snapping fingers, slowly begins to stamp out his ritualistic movements. Bates, an insecure Englishman who has been led from one calamity to another by the irrepressible Zorba, follows uncertainly, then for the first time in the film begins to gain confidence, and at picture's close the two men, side by side, arms over each other's shoulders, create a timeless image of human joy and triumph over iniquity.

DOCTOR ZHIVAGO, 1965

The hero is married but passionately loves another woman. They are forced to part through circumstances of war and by virtue of his familial situation. It is years until he sees her again. He is on a streetcar in a city and he catches sight of her on a crowded sidewalk from the window of his tram. She has been the sole obsession of his life, and he has lost her, so now he rises swiftly from his seat and exits onto the street. He starts to follow after her, but before he can get very far, before he can even call her name, he sustains a sudden heart attack and, grasping and clutching himself, his reason for existence having slipped from his grasp, he slumps to the pavement and dies. The actors are Omar Sharif and Julie Christie and the picture is *Doctor Zhivago*.

THE IPCRESS FILE, 1965

◎◎◎◎◎◎◎◎◎◎◎◎◎◎◎◎◎◎◎◎◎◎◎

In Sidney J. Furie's *The Ipcress File*, there is a brilliant death scene beneath changing stop lights at a busy London intersection on a late, wet afternoon. When the lights go green all the waiting vehicles roar off—all save one. A solitary car remains, deathly still, on the roadway. The head-and-shoulders silhouette of the lone driver (a Scotland Yard man), as seen through the rear window, remains perfectly upright and normal, in the same pose in which we last saw him scant moments before when he pulled up his car to wait for the lights to change. We are momentarily perplexed. Then a quick shot of the driver's open-eyed, puzzled face, a red bullet hole in his temple, gives us our answer.

The concept of this sequence is not original to Furie. Fritz Lang did it in 1932 when he made *The Last Will of Dr. Mabuse*. Whether Furie knew of this precedent or not, I cannot say, but I can say that his version was better than Lang's, and it was that shot through the rear window toward the silhouette of the motionless driver that did it.

BONNIE AND CLYDE, 1967

⊚①①①①①①①①①①①①①①①①①①①①⊚

Because of its irreverence for social mores and taboos, its approach to sex which stresses the problems rather than the triumphs, its uninhibited camerawork which runs from fast frame to slow motion, its concern for historical period as that period is remembered rather than as it was actually lived, its sense of changing times and human anachronism, Arthur Penn's *Bonnie and Clyde* is a landmark in modern cinema. The climactic shot of Warren Beatty's body being riddled by bullets and falling in agonizingly slow motion—his hair flowering in the sunlight—and colliding gently with the brown earth, coupled with Faye Dunaway's slow-jerking spasms as she is hit over and over in the front seat of the car, is one of the most awesome scenes of its kind ever filmed.

THE GRADUATE, 1967

⊚⊚⊚⊚⊚⊚⊚⊚⊚⊚⊚⊚⊚⊚⊚⊚⊚⊚⊚⊚⊚⊚

There is a dandy moment near the end of *The Graduate*, Mike Nichols' film about coming of age in America's upper middle class, in which Dustin Hoffman, alone, and like a latter-day Fairbanks, captures the girl he loves (Katharine Ross) right from under the nose of the man to whom she has just said "I do."

The sequence, located in a very modern West Coast church, has shades of Preston Sturges about it, particularly in the ears-nose-arm-and-hair pulling in the church foyer when groom, best man, parents, in-laws, and wedding guests all get in on the act in attempting to stop Hoffman from escaping with the bride. And our hero would not have been successful had it not been for a stiff, stout wooden cross which he seizes from its wall moorings and uses to fight off the angry crowd and to jam the glass doors for his final, and successful, escape.

The couple board a bus and we last see them, while fellow passengers gawk curiously at them, sitting in a rear seat, flushed with the excitement of the battle they have been through, and staring off into an undefined future.

A rear shot of the bus moving away from us, and the film comes to an end. But we are still thinking of the scene with the cross.

2001: A SPACE ODYSSEY, 1968

⊚⊚⊚⊚⊚⊚⊚⊚⊚⊚⊚⊚⊚⊚⊚⊚⊚⊚⊚⊚⊚⊚⊚⊚

The moment before the intermission in Stanley Kubrick's *2001: A Space Odyssey* is a point of extraordinarily high drama. We share the concern of Keir Dullea and Gary Lockwood that their spaceship robot, Hal (voice by Douglas Rain), possesses an unprecedented power of reasoning and that he may be trying to take control of their craft. So when they slip into a locked chamber (so that Hal will not be able to hear them) to reveal their feelings and thoughts to each other and to plot Hal's overthrow, we are delighted they are taking action before it is too late. But as they converse we become aware of something extremely unnerving: Hal's electronic "eye" watching them through the window of their sealed compartment. As the camera cuts to a giant close-up of their mouths in quiet dialogue, we realize in horror that Hal *can read their lips!*

THE WILD BUNCH, 1969

⊚⊛⊚⊛⊚⊛⊚⊛⊚⊛⊚⊛⊚⊛⊚⊛⊚⊛⊚⊛⊚

Sam Peckinpah's death scenes in the opening street ambush and in the final showdown with the Mexican soldiers in *The Wild Bunch* are terrifying in their visual horror, and yet, because of the slow-motion device employed to record them, become a gruesomely poetic series of screen images. Rifles and shotguns are discharged at close range, bodies twist up into the air, fold up, their faces bloodied, parts of their backs blown away, and crumple to the earth. Peckinpah thus uses a lyrical, poetic technique to highlight the horror of death in battle, and while some of his material, such as the examples given here, is repellent to many viewers, one cannot ignore the pure cinema of such sequences. *The Wild Bunch*, in my personal estimation, from its marvelous opening credits (images of William Holden and gang, attired as soldiers, riding down the main street of a post-turn-of-the-century western town, and then converting to a series of dark, static sketches of these men for main title purposes) to its ultimate showdown when Holden and his men (Ben Johnson, Ernest Borgnine, et al.) march to their doom, is probably one of the ten greatest pictures ever made in the U.S.A.

BUTCH CASSIDY
AND THE SUNDANCE KID, 1969

⊚⊚⊚⊚⊚⊚⊚⊚⊚⊚⊚⊚⊚⊚⊚⊚⊚⊚⊚⊚⊚⊚⊚

George Roy Hill's production of *Butch Cassidy and the Sundance Kid* is marvelous cinema, one of the finest Westerns of its kind, and the last shot ranks with the screen greats.

Here, Butch and Sundance (Paul Newman and Robert Redford) are hiding in a building surrounded by Bolivian soldiers, and rather than be taken alive, they charge on foot out into the brilliant sunlight of the small-town square, firing their six-shooters as they run. Hundreds of rifles, aimed down at them from surrounding rooftops, discharge volley after volley of bullets, but the image of the two outlaws has already gone into an incredible freeze frame which catches them at their zenith of violence and glory, the camera finally tracking away from them, gunfire in echo in the background, the transition to legend fully achieved.

The Seventies

We now come to the most difficult decade to chronicle, a decade not yet over. While the seventies have not been without impressive cinematic moments, I am still too close to the films to know whether or not they are the kind that will live with me. But there are a few that would appear to be fairly safe guesses, mainly from the early seventies, and one or two more recently, and I shall describe these.

One thing has become apparent to me, and doubtless to you if you have been reading this book chronologically, and this is that my magic moments are growing fewer with each decade since the peak forties. Part of the reason is the fact that the major studios and independent film makers have turned out fewer and fewer pictures each decade. Perhaps another reason is that I am a good deal older now than when I discovered movies for myself in the early thirties, have seen an awful lot of them, and have become somewhat jaded. Certainly I perceive a good deal of repetition, not only in a growing number of remakes, but in ideas and techniques. One of the hallmarks of a true magic moment in films must surely be a sense of freshness, newness, uniqueness. Due to the sheer preponderance of movies released in Canada and the United States in the last fifty years alone there are bound to be repetitions of an enormous order and possibly this sheer quantity is at last beginning to exert a numbing effect on my psyche.

But I fear that the main reason might well be that the magic is really going out of the movies. The late Henri Langlois, curator of the French Cinémathèque in Paris, suggested a few years ago that we may be in the process of experiencing the "death of cinema"—that movies as we have known them might not outlast the next decade. I have no notion what M. Langlois believed would succeed the movies. I expect home TV screens will increase in size and that much of what we see in the cinema today will be transferred to the family set. Perhaps movie theaters as we know them will become as few in number as legitimate theaters in each city and will convert to a total immersion experience induced by holography or some other complete 3-D sensation in which the "tidal wave" in the big spectacular will actually wash right over and through its audience in a sea of light, and in underwater sequences the fish will swim right past and around our heads. In such a cinema, we would be completely and totally *in* the picture.

All of this is pure conjecture. Each art has its doom-sayers just as it has its prophets of optimism. But the fact remains that magic moments for me are getting fewer and fewer and harder to find as the decades advance, and I somehow do not think I am alone in this impression. Look at the critical reaction to the remakes of *Lost Horizon, King Kong, A Star Is Born,* and *The Wages of Fear* (*Sorcerer*), to name only four of an alarming number of new versions of older films. In every case it was agreed with an amazing unanimity—the old magic was gone, the touches and sparks that once fired our imaginations were no longer present.

A final explanation is more difficult for me to write about because it probes into areas I would much rather leave in the dark. Perhaps, on the whole, movies have really grown up, become more mature, more sophisticated, while I haven't changed, haven't grown up. Perhaps the things I have always loved most in movies—things I call magic moments—were mainly fanciful and naïve clusters of film frames, odd bits of editing, ingenious camera angles and movements, freakish flights of a director's, a writer's imagination that were really rather capricious and cute and not too far removed from the sawdust and circus side shows that the movies grew up with in their beginnings.

Perhaps I am still looking for my childhood in motion pictures, a childhood that is no longer there.

The truth, if there is one, is probably a mixture of all the foregoing explanations. One thing we do know is that distance *does* lend enchantment. Conceivably in thirty years the seventies will mysteriously seem to contain far more magic moments than I can remotely imagine at present.

The seventies—the age of the giant multi-national corporations and giant unions, of supertankers and superaircraft and the superhiatus before the colonization of outer space actually begins, of the *Deep Throat* syndrome run to lunacy on the screens of the continent, of the extreme conflicts in values as represented by *Looking for Mr. Goodbar* and *Close Encounters of the Third Kind*, of the big shock horrors of *Jaws* and *The Exorcist* and the tiny glories of *Roseland*, of movie remakes and unprecedented nostalgia, of the moral dilemmas of *The Godfather* and *Apocalypse Now*, of the vanished flower children of the sixties and the hippie-become-bank tellers of today, of the corporate way, of hijacking and global blackmail, of the tarnished knighthood of American idealism, of the French-English schism in Canada that seems utterly without solution, of advancing computerization and the birth of a new harmony between man and technology, and of an ever mounting puzzlement about who we are, where we've come from, and where we're going . . .

So here they are for what they are worth, my magic moments of the seventies.

MON ONCLE ANTOINE, 1970

@@@@@@@@@@@@@@@@@@@@@@@@

Mon Oncle Antoine was directed by Claude Jutra and, together with Don Shebib's *Goin Down the Road* (1971), is at the top of Canada's achievements in the cinema.

The film is sharply etched nostalgia, a pathos-comedy portrait of a boy and a community during the twenties in the Lac St. Jean region of Quebec at a time when the boy is in the process of coming of age. An asbestos mine, owned and operated by an English-Canadian family, is the key source of income for the inhabitants of the area, who are French-Canadian. My favorite scene among many fine moments offered by this picture reveals one whole slice of the historic attitude of the French-Canadian toward the English factor, an attitude molded over the decades by political and economic exploitation and by gross misunderstanding.

The setting is the main street of the town, and the time is Christmas Day. The scene concerns the annual ritual of the English-Canadian mill owner who drives his horse-powered sleigh, full of meager-looking presents, up and down and around the main street and tosses the presents toward the doorsteps of his employees. Clearly designed for the kiddies, the slender gifts are nevertheless thrown in a brusque, arrogant manner by a man in a great fur hat and coat who has a pipe clenched stubbornly between his teeth and whose face is all coldness and disdain, with impatience and solemnity thrown in for good measure. Watching his tight, hard, abrupt way with the reins of his two horses is almost enough in itself to indicate precisely how he runs his mill. The faces of the townspeople shown in close-ups, mute and still, behind their windows or in doorways, and the silent faces of the children, these bear testimony to the quality of the event being witnessed.

The sequence ends with our young hero and a chum tossing snowballs at the two horses and sending the mine owner, in a wild rush of hooves and flying snow, off up the street and out of sight.

Our two lads walk along the street in the wake of the excitement they have caused like two Roman centurions home from a victorious campaign. Then our young hero spies the pretty, smiling face of a girl he has begun to "notice" during the time of our story. She is standing at the corner of her porch watching him. He smiles back and in his expression of warmth and newly discovered love all memory of the momentous events of the preceding minutes fades. He is Everyboy and life is now bursting with joy and promise all around him.

LITTLE BIG MAN, 1971

⊚⊚⊚⊚⊚⊚⊚⊚⊚⊚⊚⊚⊚⊚⊚⊚⊚⊚⊚⊚⊚⊚⊚

Chief Dan George walks to his tribal burial ground to die near the end of *Little Big Man*, Arthur Penn's classic of 1971, and our hearts mourn in sadness with his adopted son, Dustin Hoffman, who is standing by his side as he lies down upon a blanket, closes his eyes, and awaits the end. The moment is poignant because the old chief has become an indelible part of our lives through the unfolding of this long, picaresque tale that spans one hundred and twenty years, from pre-Custer times to the present. The only thing is—he doesn't die as he expects.

With snowflakes dropping gently on his face, he opens his eyes and says to Hoffman, "Am I still here?" And so, it appears, he is.

Disappointed, realizing his time hasn't come as he had expected, he arises, puts an arm over Hoffman's shoulders, and walks with him back down the mountainside toward his village, the pair receding from our view in successive "distance dissolves," the old chief mumbling until his voice can no longer be heard about a number of things including rumors that one of his squaws copulates with horses.

THE FRENCH CONNECTION, 1971

⊚⊚⊚⊚⊚⊚⊚⊚⊚⊚⊚⊚⊚⊚⊚⊚⊚⊚⊚⊚⊚⊚⊚

Following the cinesteps of *Bullitt* but going into a more frenetic gear, the car chase in *The French Connection* is wildly exciting, this time pitting a car, driven by a tough, semi-psychopathic detective, Gene Hackman, against an elevated train.

Hackman's horrendous drive is shot mostly from his point of view and takes the camera on maddening swerves and skids down the long aisle of girder posts underneath the scaffolding of a New York elevated subway while an express roars sickeningly overhead. Part of the tense joy lies in watching Hackman's portrayal of "Popeye" Doyle, the most uncool of all cop heroes, banging his fists on his dashboard like an angry child at every delay and frustration.

AND NOW FOR SOMETHING COMPLETELY DIFFERENT, 1972

✪◎◎◎◎◎◎◎◎◎◎◎◎◎◎◎◎◎◎◎✪

One of the funniest moments I can ever remember occurs in the Monty Python Flying Circus film, *And Now for Something Completely Different*. It is the scene in which a man appears on a night club stage with his "singing mice" act. What we see in the camera's frame is a man bringing in a large tray whose sides are about three inches high, thus obscuring from our view the mice that are inside. He places the tray on a stand table, bows to his audience, picks up two large wooden mallets, and after cuing the orchestra into the first few bars of "Three Blind Mice" commences to wallop the wooden mallets down into the "contents" of the tray. Each whack is accompanied by a brief, piercing screech, the very sound you would imagine a mouse making in its death throes. But the screeches have a harmony, and the harmony is "Three Blind Mice."

CLOCKWORK ORANGE, 1972

Stanley Kubrick's opulent, satiric journey into the social and moral decay of our world a few years hence—*Clockwork Orange* —contains several moments of high, black cinema, all of them revolting us by the nature of their content while at the same time infusing us with a sense of exultation over the sheer movie moxie of the scenes presented.

In one scene that commingles horror and pathos (and is a grimly sardonic send-up of a scene from a famous Hollywood musical of the fifties) the viewer is put through a wringer of bizarrely conflicting emotions. Anti-hero Malcolm MacDowell and his two slavish aides—a hooligan street gang trio of freakishly sophisticated bent—break into the home of a writer and his wife and proceed to rape the woman in front of her husband, all the while kicking him by slow degrees into insensibility. What gives this utterly disgusting scene its distinction is the style in which the sequence is managed. MacDowell dances "Singin' in the Rain" like a veritable Gene Kelly, punctuating his fancy stepping with kicks into the belly of the writer, who lies prone upon the floor writhing in agony, and swats his cane across the face of the wife, who is being held upright by the two thugs, her dress having been slit open from top to bottom in preparation for the rape.

The scene is gay and light and rhythmic; the scene is one of horrifyingly sadistic violence; the scene is a freakish tour down movieland's memory lane; it is a snippet of grim fairy-tale lore à la the Marquis de Sade, 1983.

LAST TANGO IN PARIS, 1973

Due to some incredibly explicit sex scenes, the variety of the sex acts performed, as well as an animal sensuousness rare on the screen till then, *Last Tango in Paris*, directed by Bernardo Bertolucci, achieved uncommon notoriety. What is often forgotten among all of one's turbulent memories of encounters between Marlon Brando and Maria Schneider is a sequence in the dim confines of a funeral chamber in which Mr. Brando maintains a brooding vigil beside the coffin containing the dead body of his wife, Helen.

The sequence is described in retrospect with Brando's off-screen voice telling Maria Schneider of how (despite his wife's numerous and flaunting betrayals and her hatred for him and the hell he experienced every day that he lived with her) now that she was gone he realized his utter aloneness, and how much he grieved her loss because, in all the universe, she was the only human companion he had, his only friend, his only love.

PAT GARRETT AND BILLY THE KID, 1973

In Sam Peckinpah's marred but excellent *Pat Garrett and Billy the Kid* there is a short scene that really doesn't relate to the main action, and yet it produced upon this viewer a feeling of timelessness, humanity, family-togetherness, loneliness, fear-in-the-dark and violence-about-to-erupt-but-didn't primitiveness, human courage and protectiveness that suited the haunting mood of the film and gave it real place and period.

The scene I am referring to occurs when Pat Garrett is lying against the trunk of a tree on a riverbank taking shots at a bottle floating on the water. It is dusk, and out of the gathering gloom comes a small, flat-bottomed river boat coasting gently with the current. A big, broad-shouldered, bearded man with long black hair, broad-brimmed hat, dark clothes and boots has been poling the squat craft, but at the sound of Garrett's six-shooter, he picks up his rifle and proceeds to aim it in the general direction of the bank. Each man remains tense and poised. The man in the boat sends a bullet winging close to Garrett's head, but Garrett does not respond. The tensions and sense of aloneness and strangeness continue as the two men remain immobile and alert, each seemingly waiting for the other to do something, yet somehow respecting the other's silence. The big man's family, several wide-eyed, fair-haired children, huddle together behind the pile of goods on the boat that's wrapped in canvas sacking while the father maintains his protective vigil, and in this fashion they drift by and disappear into the night.

LENNY, 1974

◎◎◎◎◎◎◎◎◎◎◎◎◎◎◎◎◎◎◎◎◎

Valerie Perrine gives Dustin Hoffman a birthday gift in *Lenny*, directed by Bob Fosse, that sends him into paroxysms of delight. Certainly I, as a viewer, have not been able to get over it.

Seated on the floor of a room, her legs seductively bunched up so that her arms and chin are resting on her knees, surrounded by dozens of bouquets of birthday flowers, she is attired only in a garter. Her face, her figure, the joyous-free mood of the moment create the loveliest image of sensual charm in movieland.

THE MAN WHO WOULD BE KING, 1975

The death of Sean Connery in *The Man Who Would Be King,* directed by John Huston, evokes a romantic sense of tragedy which I have scarcely seen on the screen since the thirties and forties when people actually died for their country in movie scenarios.

In this age of cynicism about things political and governmental, it seems no longer fashionable to do this, but in that more innocent age when Gary Cooper gave up his life exploding an ammunition dump in *The Lives of a Bengal Lancer* or James Cagney sacrificed his in *The Fighting 69th* or Sam Jaffe fell from the Kali's tower, bugle slung around him, in *Gunga Din,* such acts were mourned by a tear-stained audience.

In *The Man Who Would Be King* Danny and Peachy (Sean Connery and Michael Caine) play two Cockney, devil-may-care soldiers of the Queen with a British regiment in India. Their imaginations set afire by promises of untold wealth, they seek and find at the end of an epic journey into India's far-flung northwestern frontier a near legendary kingdom by the name of Kafiristan. Here, through a combination of bravery and sheer accident, Connery comes to be regarded by the inhabitants as a god and hence becomes king with Caine as his aide. Connery actually develops into quite a wise and good monarch, an interesting twist on the maxim about the corrupting influence of power, but in the end his all too real mortality shows itself and he is dethroned and condemned to death.

The climactic sequence is shot on the brink of a great chasm which is spanned by a slender, gently drooping rope bridge. In a brief battle the supporters of Danny and Peachy have been killed and now the crowds hem in our two protagonists on all sides. Only the path to the sacrificial bridge is left open and Connery knows what he must do.

He bids farewell to his friend, who is powerless to help him, and attired in full kingly raiment, walks out onto the bridge. Then, in one of those moments of imperishable screen grandeur and tragic dignity, he grasps the rope railing and, looking back steadily at Caine, awaits the end. Great swords begin chopping at the ropes and the strains of "The Minstrel Boy" grow and flood the screen. Connery's face and form begin to jar in the screen frame before us due to the shuddering blows of the swords, but his eyes remain on his friend until the giant bridge rips apart and he falls from view.

COUSIN COUSINE, 1976

◎◎◎◎◎◎◎◎◎◎◎◎◎◎◎◎◎◎◎◎◎◎◎◎

We are now positively too close to the present for rational judgment, but I must include one last moment, if only to give this book, in the tradition of cinema in its grandest days and a vogue which interestingly enough has returned, a happy ending.

Cousin Cousine, directed by Jean-Charles Tacchella, tells its story of extramarital love ironically in terms of the Christmas and birthday parties and other social events of a large French family of parents, children, aunts, uncles, nieces and nephews, and, of course, cousins. The hero and heroine (Marie-Christine Barrault and Victor Lamoux) are two cousins who are members of separate families and who lead reasonably unhappy married lives. They get to know each other through force of circumstance and slowly, unrelentingly, fall into complete, passionate love. But they refuse to hide their affair and hence become a family scandal.

In the end, at a large party which even features a magician who saws in half one of the more dominant female characters in the film—one of the aunts if memory serves me (Ginette Garcin, I think)—just as we are beginning to believe the romantic pair will decide to part and each return to his and her former spouse, they surprise us and everyone in the film by leaving their respective families for good and running away together. As you can imagine all is tragi-comic bedlam and confusion on the screen, with everyone running in every direction and the camera running with them.

But in a last unforgettably funny shot the camera peeks back into the parlor, where about ten minutes earlier the aunt was sawed in half by the magician. And there she still lies, astride a table in the deserted parlor, forgotten by everyone in the film and almost by us, her blond head protruding from one end of a box, her legs protruding from the other half of the box, the two halves clearly separated by a good foot or two of space where the saw has done its magic work.

"Hey—where is everybody?" her meek voice asks. "Where is everybody?"

Epilogue

I have come to the present and therefore to the end of my memories, but because by now it will have become apparent to you as it has to me that the real meaning of what constitutes a magic moment in the cinema is elusive and difficult to define and exists in a mental never-never land, perhaps it is most fitting to round off this journey by a flashback to movie moments that I once experienced at some distant time but have never been able to retrace or locate.

These I classify as my great lost moments of movie magic. My Aunt Georgy, now in her nineties, loves to recount the day in the late twenties or early thirties when she was out shopping with my mother and discovered me wandering up Main Street from the Weston Theatre bawling my eyes out. I had seen a Tom Mix Western—at least we all *think* it was a Tom Mix Western—and even though it undoubtedly had a happy ending, a scene occurring earlier in its running length had so affected me that I had been unable to recover. Tears streaming, I was hauled into my aunt's Durante and taken home. On the way I described the scene that had hit me so traumatically.

Tom had been lost in the desert for days without water or food. Some villains had left him in this state and had driven off his horse, Tony. Staggering and rolling down sand dunes, he searched for a water hole, but always the same monotonous wasteland loomed ahead. Then, when all hope appeared lost, when the anxiety within me had just about achieved the breaking point, Tom stumbled upon his horse.

Tony! Safety at last!

I can still remember Tom crawling up to his horse and clawing, almost agonizingly, for the canteen that was slung down from the saddle. Gripping a stirrup he somehow managed to pull himself to his feet, and there, abreast of the saddle, so riven with thirst that he could barely co-ordinate his fingers into removing the stopper, Tom finally tilted the canteen to his parched mouth, and we the audience licked our lips in anticipation of the cool water that would pour forth.

But no such gratification was going to be ours. Something poured from the mouth of the canteen, but it was not water. *It was sand!* The rascally villains had played their final trick on poor Tom.

I can still see and hear Tom Mix spitting out the sand. I can still see the tiny granules on his tongue. I can still see his face of despair as he leaned weakly against Tony, one arm over the saddle, the other at his side, his canteen slipping out of his fingers.

I think Tom mounted Tony and struggled to a cabin on the edge of the desert, but I can't remember. And he must have got the bad guys before the fade-out. This really didn't matter to me. The horrible moment of the sand in the canteen had been too much.

And I was still crying when my aunt and my mother found me on Main Street on my way home.

One moment that was so lost it did not occur to me until about a year after I had begun my first draft of this book is contained in what I suspect was an early "B" film. Title unknown to me now, the picture is about a great racing driver who is temporarily blinded by gangsters who do not want him to compete in the big race and win.

Somehow the driver knows he is going to lose his sight for a couple of days, and for reasons too bizarre to attempt to re-fathom does not want to let anyone know he knows. But he is still determined to win the race.

With his last few hours of eyesight on the day before the big contest, he drives the track and practices a counting system so that on specific numbers he will know where to turn and by how much. Then comes the race and one of movieland's great moments: the hero driving stone blind, and counting, and turning on cue, and driving perilously close to collisions, and counting, and sometimes miscalculating by a fraction of a second and nearly crashing out, but regaining direction and roaring on.

Finally he blasts across the finish line in victory, then smashes (albeit safely) through a fence because he hadn't taken his counting past that point.

There is a cartoon in existence whose name I do not know, although it is probably called *The Snowman*. My family and I saw it over ten years ago one Saturday morning on television and its impact is still with us. It does something with a carrot at the end which, in light of a ubiquitous Bugs Bunny ritual, earns the moment a place among movie greats.

The cartoon was done in simple black and white, but in full animation, and ran the traditional eight minutes. Its story starts with a small boy on a hill in winter building a snowman complete with top hat, scarf, coals for eyes, and a carrot for its nose. After the boy departs for home, the snowman mysteriously comes to life—I seem to recall a freak lightning storm and something of a Frankenstein implication—and soon makes friends with a passing rabbit. The pair cavort and have a great time, and soon the snowman begins to wish their friendship could last indefinitely and starts to dream the great dream of transcending winter and actually experiencing a summer's day, something no snowman had ever done before in the whole long history of snowmen.

One day the pair encounter an icehouse with a special timing mechanism on its refrigeration doorlock. The snowman suddenly gets the idea that the icehouse will provide him with the very means he has been seeking of staying alive so that he can have a rendezvous with his pal, the rabbit, on the first of July when summer will be in full bloom. Then, as spring approaches, he takes temporary leave from his friend and stores himself away in the icehouse, where he has set the timer to open the door a bit before noon on July the first. Spring comes and converts to summer and finally the first of July arrives.

Out steps the snowman like a creature returning to earth from the dead. He laughs and skips and jumps across the fields toward

239

the hill to make his noon hour appointment, enjoying the sun and the blue sky and the warmth and the yellow flowers, a miracle of nature totally unknown to him till now.

As he waits on the familiar hilltop for his old friend, the rabbit, the warmth from the sun increases and, to his horror, he begins to melt. The rabbit, a tardy chap, is late, and the snowman can do nothing to withhold the inevitable. And so he continues to melt and, sinking slowly toward the ground, "dies" on this beautiful summer day, grateful to have been permitted to see summer, if only for a short time, yet saddened at not having seen his friend again.

A little while later the rabbit comes by and waits for the snowman. When he does not arrive the rabbit reasons his pal had probably forgotten the rendezvous, shrugs, and decides to push off. Looking down he spies a carrot on the grass, picks it up, and is last seen trotting away chewing quite contentedly.

Another lost moment relates to a Western I saw one night around 1929 or 1930 with my father and a friend of his, a golf pro named Bill McWilliams. The title is long gone from memory, and the star as well, although something tells me it was Bob Steele. Then again, it could have been Bob Baker. No matter, it was a black-and-white, 4-by-3-screen, "B"-class Western, and it contained an unforgettable bit of stuntwork involving the hero, a lariat, and an open-air touring car with two villains in the rear seat.

The ten-gallon-hatted hero stood on a spur of rock on a cliffside whirling his rope round and round over his head. Down the road came the touring car with the two henchmen in the rear seat. How the hero escaped being seen I'll never know, but just as the car passed beneath the rock, he hurled his rope in a brisk downward motion and settled its noose over the torsos of the two badmen. Then he drew the rope abruptly back, and the two men were literally yanked right out of their seat and onto the road. It was a moment of modest spectacle, and one I shall always cherish.

I had always thought the following vanished sequence occurred in Will Rogers' film *Judge Priest*, but when recently my wife and

I attended a revival of that film at the Ontario Film Theatre in Toronto, the scene in question was nowhere to be found.

As memory has it two men meet in buggies on dark, midnight crossroads. Their lanterns only serve to highlight, in the intense gloom that shrouds them, their lifelong hatred for each other. Sharp words are exchanged, they begin to grapple, and one of the two, in order to defend himself, picks up an object and hits the other man over the head with it. An ordinary object and the scene would never have been imprinted so indelibly upon my mind. But this was no ordinary object. What the chap had picked up from the seat of the buggy to hit the other fellow over the head with was nothing less than a *Bible*. And on the screens of the early thirties, that was *some* object to hit one over the head with.

Another old, old memory is that of a great dining table in a castle or mansion or ancient château with highbacked chairs around it. I think there were thirteen chairs in all, which gives rise to the possibility that the film was *The Thirteenth Chair* (Tod Browning, 1929), but I have not been able to find this film to check. At any rate, when a set of oddly assorted guests had assembled and commenced their meal—the host, I seem to recall, wore a turban—the lights went out, and when they went on again the occupant of a particular chair (the thirteenth?) was missing and the chair starkly vacant. The lights had only been out for two or three seconds, thus where could the missing guest be? How could he vanish?

This event occurred throughout the film with different sets of guests until, in the denouement, we discovered that the back of the "fatal" chair, which rested against a stone wall, contained a trap door and that each successive occupant had been catapulted by this means out of the room to his or her grisly fate. Something tells me that C. Henry Gordon, probably my favorite of all villains, wore the turban, but I cannot be sure. . . .

INDEX OF MOVIE TITLES